HENDRIK M. RUITENBEEK was born in 1928 in Leiden, Holland. A distinguished scholar and psychotherapist, he was awarded a doctorate in sociology and law from the University of Leiden, following which he received extensive psychological and psychoanalytic training in the United States and abroad. Dr. Ruitenbeek has subsequently taught at various colleges. At present he is practicing psychoanalysis in New York City, and is also on the faculty of the American Institute for Psychotherapy and Psychoanalysis. He is the editor or author of several books, among which are *PSYCHOANALYSIS AND CONTEMPORARY AMERICAN CULTURE, VARIETIES OF PERSONALITY THEORY, VARIETIES OF MODERN SOCIAL THEORY, THE INDIVIDUAL AND THE CROWD, PSYCHOANALYSIS AND EXISTENTIAL PHILOSOPHY, FREUD AND AMERICA, THE MALE MYTH*, and *FREUD AS WE KNEW HIM*.

THE NEW GROUP THERAPIES, also by Dr. Ruitenbeek, is available in an Avon Discus edition.

Other Discus books by
Hendrik Ruitenbeek

THE NEW GROUP THERAPIES   27995   1.95

PSYCHOTHERAPY:
WHAT IT'S ALL ABOUT

HENDRIK M. RUITENBEEK

 A DISCUS BOOK/PUBLISHED BY AVON BOOKS

AVON BOOKS
A division of
The Hearst Corporation
959 Eighth Avenue
New York, New York 10019

Copyright © 1976 by R & M Associates.
Library of Congress Catalog Card Number: 76-26765

All rights reserved, which includes the right
to reproduce this book or portions thereof in
any form whatsoever. For information address
Avon Books.

ISBN: 0-380-00811-4

First Discus Printing, September, 1976

DISCUS TRADEMARK REG. U.S. PAT. OFF. AND IN
OTHER COUNTRIES, MARCA REGISTRADA,
HECHO EN U.S.A.

Printed in the U.S.A.

For James Bell
"A talent to amuse"

Noel Coward

"er is geen langere liefde
dan die van de glimlach"

Hans Lodeizen

Contents

	FOREWORD	9
	PREFACE	15
Chapter 1	Psychotherapy and Who Does It	23
	What are the ground rules of therapy and psychoanalysis?	
Chapter 2	What Do I Need?	39
Chapter 3	What Can You Do for Me?	51
Chapter 4	Talking to Your Therapist: Free Association and Dreams	67
Chapter 5	How Do I Feel About My Therapist?	87
Chapter 6	How Long Is This Going to Last?: Diagnosis and Prognosis	103
Chapter 7	Should I Get Into a Group?	119
Chapter 8	Why Do Therapists Charge So Much?	129
Appendix I	The Main Psychoanalytic Schools	141
Appendix II	Where to Go for Help in Finding an Analyst	147
	BIBLIOGRAPHY	151
	INDEX	156

Foreword

This small book does not pretend to be a study of psychoanalysis, but rather its purpose is to provide the informed reader with glimpses of the psychotherapeutic process.

Many thanks to Dr. Richard McConchie for his invaluable help in getting the manuscript into shape while in its final stages.

DR. HENDRIK M. RUITENBEEK

"I didn't say there was nothing *better*," the King replied. "I said there was nothing *like* it." Alice did not venture to deny.

—Lewis Carroll
Through the Looking-Glass

PSYCHOTHERAPY:

WHAT IT'S ALL ABOUT

Preface

Freud's student and biographer, the English psycho-analyst Ernest Jones, once remarked that Freud's *Three Contributions to the Theory of Sex* was probably his most original contribution to psychoanalytic science after *The Interpretation of Dreams*. To these I would like to add Freud's papers on technique, which set forth the general principles by which the therapeutic situation is governed. It is surprising that Freud never wrote a general handbook on the technique of psychoanalysis, although James Strachey notes that he planned to do so. Ultimately Freud abandoned the project, and the bulk of his writings on the technique of psychoanalysis is found in a series of papers published between 1911 and 1915, with the exception of two final papers published in 1937, two years before his death: "Analysis Terminable and Interminable" and "Constructions in Analysis."

Reading Freud's papers on technique today, some sixty years after they were written, one is amazed by their relevance. Additionally, their clear but literary style and uncomplicated presentation of basic concepts make them readily understandable to the layman. But while many of Freud's original recommendations and observations on the analytic situation are still valid and need little elaboration or revision, it is clear that others are outdated and that new papers on technique are required to deal with the changes in the analytic situation and the analysand that have occurred since Freud's day, in terms of the roles and life situations of both patients and analysts.

Since the publication of Freud's papers on technique, many theorists have tried to extend the parameters of psychoanalytic techniques. Most of their works—primarily those by Otto Fenichel, Karl Menninger, and Ralph Greenson—are mainly intended as textbooks for psychoanalysts and thus employ psychoanalytic terminology freely. Compared to the straightforward and well-written papers of Freud, they are frequently tedious to prospective analysts and laymen alike.

This is not to say that there are no popular books on psychoanalysis or psychotherapy around. On the contrary, they are far too numerous and generally far too popular. They rarely deal with the therapeutic situation from the point of view of the prospective patient; nor do they often delve into the feelings of the therapist toward his patient—in more technical terms, his countertransference.

It would be presumptuous to say that I have improved upon Freud's contributions to psychoanalytic technique in this book, but hopefully I have put them in the context of psychotherapy and psychoanalysis *anno* 1976, and have reinterpreted them with the image of the contemporary patient and therapist in mind. Needless to say, I also borrowed from the newer therapeutic schools that seem to be sprouting like mushrooms with each successive year. I have drawn

16

especially upon the rich resources of the existential school of psychoanalysis. I have also traced some of the active therapies that are so popular today back to those two brilliant pupils of Freud: Sándor Ferenczi and Otto Rank.

In the course of writing this book I have been reinforced in my belief that psychoanalysis will continue both as a therapy and as a philosophy for understanding the larger social order. It is probably the best tool we have so far developed for handling and interpreting our complex interpersonal relationships and our interactions with our environment.

For those who feel that psychoanalysis has exhausted its potential for further innovation, this book will be a disappointment. Psychoanalysis is still advancing and many people continue to benefit from its philosophy and methods of treatment. Psychoanalysis has not stood still in the half century since patients visited Professor Freud's office in Vienna at Berggasse 19 five or six times a week. At that time psychoanalysis, or for that matter any kind of psychotherapy, was very much a private affair (the French word *privé* is a more accurate descriptive term) that one did not talk about. Today psychoanalysis has been demystified and has gained respectability in the process. In America at least, psychoanalysis has become a recognized, openly accepted form of psychotherapy. Psychotherapy, including the broader mental health therapies such as group therapy, family therapy, community-oriented therapy, the intervention and crisis therapies, and more recently the encounter and chemotherapies, has become an important part of the middle-class picture. Although therapeutic services are available for members of the working class and the poor, such services are still extremely inadequate and fail by far to meet the emotional requirements of these groups. Ghetto therapy is still in a very experimental stage, although serious efforts are being made to remedy this situation.

One might wonder if the basic rules for the conduct of psychoanalysis as they were developed by Freud are applicable to this greatly expanded range of specialized therapies. As I will try to show in this book, these rules should not be rejected merely because they were formulated sixty years ago. Many are still applicable either wholly or in part. Others are obviously not, since the scope of psychotherapy has broadened considerably and, more important, therapists see patients who are very different from those Freud saw in Vienna early in the twentieth century.

While the wide acceptance accorded psychotherapy by Americans in general has resulted in a great deal of familiarity with psychoanalytic concepts, there is also considerable ignorance about the actual *process* of psychoanalysis or psychotherapy. And, sadly enough, even among young, beginning psychotherapists, there is often ignorance about how to handle the therapeutic situation. Nowadays, many newly trained psychotherapists come from disciplines other than psychiatry and psychology, such as sociology, anthropology, counseling, and psychiatric social work (to mention but a few), and often in the process of becoming psychotherapists they continue to place too much emphasis on what they learned previously in their particular area of specialization. Consequently, they have trouble in developing a new professional identity, that is, really seeing themselves as psychotherapists. Much of their difficulty in this respect stems from the absence of officially accredited academic programs leading to doctorates in analytic psychotherapy. As I will describe in Chapter I, the often sterile and acrimonious debates over a particular course of study to be required of a prospective psychoanalytic therapist as well as exactly who is qualified to be admitted to a given training institute have done much to retard the development of more effective therapeutic techniques and to sow confusion in the mind of the lay public.

Even after he has decided to enter some form of therapy, the prospective patient still finds himself in a rather perplexing situation. (Please note that although it is safe to assume that approximately half of all patients are women and there are many female psychotherapists, for the sake of simplicity the masculine gender is used almost exclusively throughout this book with reference to both patients and therapists.) Many patients in therapy still believe that analysis is an almost mystical method of probing the innermost recess of the mind. Quite the contrary is true. The principles and techniques of psychoanalysis are well known and have been discussed in many professional as well as nonprofessional journals, magazines, and books. However, one should not forget that each individual's therapeutic experience always differs from what one may read in a book. Every patient believes that his analysis is totally different from all others, and he is correct in this belief because each patient and consequently each therapeutic situation is unique.

This sense of uniqueness and individuality applies equally to the therapist himself. He, too, experiences the analytic situation of each of his patients as unique, and is tempted to view the analytic situation as one that is controlled and guided by him. No matter how well analyzed the therapist may be, he will still derive personal satisfaction from the relatively omnipotent role he is playing. Such are the temptations of being a therapist!

This book makes no pretense of stating the definitive rules of the game called psychotherapy but, rather, discusses the various possible rules and regulations and the possibilities and nonpossibilities of the psychoanalytic therapeutic process. It deals with problems concerning the choice of a therapist, his possible theoretical orientation and approaches to treatment, fees, missed appointments, transference, countertransference, resistance, and repression. The comments in this book are intended as a set of explanations and guidelines which will hopefully be of help to patients as well as to some beginning therapists.

Finally, it must be said that depth analysis is not for everyone. Freud did not even believe that it led to a cure *per se,* but saw it much more as a process that ultimately enables the patient to live in peace with himself, having accepted and adjusted to his personal limitations. Modern psychoanalysis, on the other hand, as represented by the neo-Freudian, existential, and object-relations schools, has gone beyond this more limited, earlier view. The contemporary analyst is often no longer satisfied with a therapy that merely enables the patient to live with his problems; rather, he tries to uncover and develop his patients' potentialities and help him to learn how to use them to better his life situation. Gone is the day when mere understanding of the dynamics of one's psychological problems was considered the criterion of success in therapy. Today's therapist strives to move beyond understanding to effect structural change in the patient's psyche and consequently to bring about a "cure" in the more generally accepted sense of the word.

—Dr. Hendrik Ruitenbeek
September, 1976

Chapter 1

PSYCHOTHERAPY
AND WHO DOES IT

So you've finally decided that you want to go to a therapist with your problems and you're wondering what steps to take. Some of your friends are "in analysis" and they have given you all sorts of advice about how to proceed. You might have read Freud's *Interpretation of Dreams* in a pocket edition and you took Psychology I in college, but you now discover that you really do not know anything about psychoanalysis.

The difference between psychoanalysis and psychotherapy is a crucial one. The literal meaning of psychoanalysis is the analysis of the psyche, while psychotherapy denotes the therapy of the psyche. In psychoanalysis the patient is confronted with a longer and more tedious process of investigating and exploring his psyche than in psychotherapy. He will go to his analyst three to five times a week and must be prepared to face four to seven years of hard work. The exploration of the psyche is by no means a pleasant ego trip. On the contrary, it is an anxiety-provoking process, often distressing but also often exhilarating. There are no quick, easy solutions to be had in this kind of analytic investigation. The term cure is somewhat irrelevant; the words growth and development are more appropriate. Insights have to be gained and worked through. Few are qualified to undertake this process to begin with, and even more important, few have the stamina to face the kind of ordeal it can become. As Freud has repeatedly pointed out, the patient presenting himself for analysis should be intelligent, able to verbalize his problems, functioning to the extent that he is able to support himself emotionally and financially, and in a larger context be in touch with the world. And since the analyst does not reassure or support the patient, the patient needs a basic ego strength to face what is involved.

Freud believed that this kind of analysis was primarily designed for neurotics and that all other character disorders, such as psychoses, were untreatable by the psychoanalytic method as he had developed it. So the prerequisites for going into this form of treatment are heavy and demanding both from the emotional and financial angles.

Contrary to what many people think, a very considerable number of neurotics still enter this kind of traditionally designed analysis. We should add that a "traditionally designed analysis" is not necessarily a Freudian analysis. Existential and neo-Freudian analysts conduct analyses that take the same length of time as those conducted by Freudians. The fact that the emphasis of these analyses is different from that of the Freudian does not mean that they are shorter.

The question whether you qualify as a candidate for psychoanalysis obviously is not going to be decided by you, as a patient, but by your prospective analyst. The only factor that might prevent you from even considering a traditional analysis might be money, since this process often requires a heavy investment of money and time.

Patients who seek psychotherapy as distinct from psychoanalysis are on the whole more interested in their therapy as a means of problem-solving. They are usually in a hurry, they want quick results, have little or no patience, and also often find it difficult to commit themselves to any psychotherapeutic process of long duration. They are usually more disturbed than the neurotic patients in psychoanalysis; often they are borderline or psychotic patients. They also seldom have the means to put themselves through the longer process of psychoanalysis. Moreover, they are poor candidates for psychoanalysis since they are not willing to submit themselves to the rather severe discipline this form of treatment demands. They cancel appointments at random and are not prepared to make any sacrifices for their psychotherapy.

For these individuals, the shorter forms of psychotherapy, which deal primarily with symptom-solving situations, are ideal, although such therapies are often a burden for the therapist involved. The therapists in such situations must be far more active and often get more involved with their patients than in the traditional analytic situation.

Admittedly many contemporary therapists believe that, given the situation of contemporary society, we cannot any longer afford the traditional type of analysis. Such therapists often refuse to see patients more than once or twice a week. This kind of therapy seems to be emerging rapidly among the middle-class and suburban population in America. The influence of the encounter therapies and the impact of the new group therapies are being acutely felt. Indeed, the encounter therapies of the last decade have sometimes erroneously created the impression that one's neuroses can be resolved in a relatively short time.

If you do decide to seek a therapist you are faced with many practical questions. There are those who call themselves psychoanalysts and have a medical degree, a Ph. D., or an M. A. Which should you choose?

Unfortunately, the field of psychoanalysis happens to be the most confused among all the professions when it comes to qualifications, background, and training.

The American Psychoanalytic Association, which is a branch of the International Psychoanalytic Association (founded by Freud) and is regarded as the most orthodox of all the professional organizations in the field, considers as professional psychoanalysts only those who have been trained in their training institutes. In contrast to other branches of the International Psychoanalytic Association, which on the Continent and in England do admit lay people to their training institutes, the A.P.A. adheres to a strict standard of admitting only medical people to its programs. All prospective trainees must have an M.D. in order to be admitted to the A.P.A. program. Often the M.D.'s have also received psychiatric training. Under no circumstances does the American Psychoanalytic Association admit psychologists or social workers to its training programs.

Other institutes have been less rigorous in their admission standards mainly because they recognize that those who are training in psychology, sociology, anthropology, and social work often make excellent candidates for psychoanalytic training. In New York City, for example, we find the National Psychological Association for Psychoanalysis (NPAP), which was founded by a pupil of Freud, Theodore Reik, who was himself denied membership in the American Psychoanalytic Association because he lacked a medical degree; the William Alanson White Institute, which admits both M.D.'s and Ph.D.'s to its program and whose orientation is primarily neo-Freudian: the Post-Graduate Center; and the American Institute for Psychotherapy and Psychoanalysis. All of them in varying degrees admit nonmedical people to their training programs. They differ in the number of hours they require the trainee to devote to his personal analysis and also have various approaches to training and supervisory analysis.

It is important that the prospective patient ascertain where his analyst received his training; that training includes a personal analysis, which is a requirement for every analyst who wants to analyze patients.

It is altogether possible that you will be referred to a psychiatrist who of course has an M.D. and has received psychiatric training; even with this training he is not qualified to practice psychoanalysis unless he has received additional training at a psychoanalytic institute and has been analyzed himself.

You might also be faced with the following situation. You will visit a man with a Ph.D. in clinical psychology and you are impressed with the school where he received the degree. But this degree alone does not qualify him to do analysis or even supportive therapy. Again, as with the psychiatrist, he has to have had training at a psychoanalytic institute and must have been analyzed himself.

The same standard also applies to social workers. Often they have done extensive clinical work in their social work practice, but that does not make them therapists or analysts.

Some of your friends might argue that you should get a medical analyst since he can prescribe drugs. You should bear in mind, however, that psychoanalysis as conceived by Freud is and was a process in which drugs should not play a role. Freud believed that the anxiety provoked in the patient by the psychoanalytic process was a productive phenomenon and that the patient should stay away from drugs. Unfortunately, with the introduction of the tranquilizing drugs in the last few decades, some analysts have used these drugs to alleviate the anxieties in their patients. Moreover, many tranquilizers are intended to be used by psychotic or borderline patients, patients who are usually poor candidates for psychotherapy and psychoanalysis.

Freud himself was very much in favor of lay analysis, or analysis conducted by nonmedical analysts. He wrote a little book in 1926 defending lay analysis,[1] a book that has been studiously ignored by the medical psychoanalytic establishment in this country. As always, Freud had great foresight and he expressed the

[1] Sigmund Freud, *The Question of Lay Analysis*, vol. XX, *The Standard Edition* (London: Hogarth Press, 1959).

hope that one day psychoanalysis would be taught at the universities as a separate discipline. In his words:

Analytic training, it is true, cuts across the field of medical education, but neither includes the other. If—which may sound fantastic today— one had to found a college of psychoanalysis, much would have to be taught in it which is also taught by the medical faculty: alongside of depth-psychology, which would always remain the principal subject, there would be an introduction to biology, as much as possible of the science of sexual life, and familiarity with the symptomatology of psychiatry. On the other hand, analytic instruction would include branches of knowledge which are remote from medicine and which the doctor does not come across in his practice: the history of civilization, mythology, the psychology of religion and the science of literature. Unless he is well at home in these subjects, an analyst can make nothing of a large amount of his material. . . . the great mass of what is taught in medical schools is of no use to him for his purposes. . . . A knowledge of the anatomy of the tarsal bones, of the constitution of the carbohydrates, of the course of the cranial nerves, a grasp of all that medicine has brought to light on bacillary exciting causes of disease and the means of combating them, on serum reactions and on neoplasms—all of this knowledge, which is undoubtedly of the highest value in itself, is nevertheless of no consequence to him; it does not concern

him; it neither helps him directly to understand a
neurosis and to cure it nor does it contribute to
a sharpening of those intellectual capacities on
which his occupation makes the greatest demands.[2]

In the selection of your analyst or therapist considerations other than training may also play a role.
Friends often refer you to their analysts because they
are satisfied with *their* treatment situation. It is also
possible that a member of your own family is already in analysis and will refer you to his analyst.
Some analysts try to stay away from these family-
referral situations. They feel that treating two or even
more members of the same family might cause serious
transference troubles. The inevitable competition for
the analyst might work counterproductively in these
analyses. Analysts have similar reservations about
treating both husband and wife, even if in separate,
individual sessions. Most analysts prefer that husband
and wife see different analysts. For the sake of ob-
jectivity on the part of the analyst and to avoid any
competitive situations, it seems wise that you select a
different analyst from your wife's or husband's.

Of course there are alternatives. You might need
marital therapy; in that case you and your husband
or wife will seek the same analyst and you will both
attend the sessions together. You should realize, however, that marital therapy is not psychoanalysis, but
a form of psychotherapy. Psychoanalysis works within

---

[2] Freud, *The Question of Lay Analysis,* p. 246.

the framework of the relationship between *one* patient and *one* analyst.

It is possible that you may already know the analyst you are about to consult professionally. You might have met him once or twice socially. Again, following Freud's advice, most analysts refuse to see friends or even acquaintances in analysis, since they feel that the previous relationship would create difficulties in the transference situation. An analyst might see a friend or acquaintance for a single consultation and advise him about the kind of analyst he might see, or put certain of his problems in some kind of perspective for him, but it should end there.

As a prospective patient, you might also wonder if you should see a male or female analyst. With the emergence of Women's Liberation there are indications that some women want to see only female analysts, and in the context of a male-oriented society this feeling is understandable. The more "progressive" female analysts, in contrast to the orthodox ones, would tend to be more sympathetic with the plight of women in society and in the family. But one of the main considerations should be whether you feel comfortable with your prospective analyst, regardless of sex.

You also might have a particular problem that would lead you to select an analyst of a particular orientation in terms of his way of thinking and philosophy of life. A tense, uptight, middle-class analyst would not be exactly the right kind of analyst for a "hippie" patient. It is especially important that young people entering analysis or psychotherapy select those analysts who are in tune with what goes on in the world of adolescents and teenagers.

Homosexuals on the whole have suffered most from bad choices in selecting their analysts. Since most heterosexual analysts in this country still embrace the pathology-and-disease concept of homosexual behavior, they have in turn done a great deal of harm to their homosexual patients. Given the complexity of the homosexual community and the often esoteric existence of many homosexuals, it would be advisable for the homosexual to seek out a therapist of the same orientation. Just recently in New York City, the Homosexual Community Counseling Center (HCCC) was founded in order to assist homosexuals who seek therapy or analysis by referring them to the proper analyst or therapist. The center has a list of qualified professionals both homosexual and heterosexual who view homosexuality as an alternative life-style and just another form of sexual behavior and not as an illness.

You also might have feelings about seeing someone who is older or younger than you are. Shopping around for a therapist is not a waste of time but a necessity. You should realize that when you enter therapy, you will be making an emotional investment as well as a financial one. And as with all investments, you have to be careful. You are going to live with the therapy or analysis for some time, and it is extremely important that you are reasonably sure that you have selected the right analyst.

Don't think that what you are about to undertake is going to be an easy process. Realize that your problems might stem from causes deeply rooted in the past and that analysis or even psychotherapy is not going to change or eliminate these causes overnight. The analytic process, no matter what the analyst's school or orientation, is a long and arduous one. There are no shortcuts, and those who will tell you that there are such shortcuts are either ignorant or irresponsible.

Many of the recommendations that Freud gave for the conduct of the psychoanalytic process are still extremely valid today. He writes, for example:

> Lengthy preliminary discussions before the beginning of the analytic treatment, previous treatment by another method and also previous acquaintance between the doctor and the patient who is to be analysed, have special disadvantageous consequences for which one must be prepared. They result in the patient's meeting the doctor with a transference attitude which is already established and which the doctor must first slowly uncover instead of having the opportunity to observe the growth and development of the transference from the outset.[3]

Another issue to be considered is summed up in the often-stated query, "Well, why can't I talk to my friends about these problems? It will cost me less!" You need to realize that talking to your friends about your problems will only temporarily relieve you of your burdens. Such talks will not *change* your life situation, nor do your friends have the insight and perception to guide you on an often tortuous journey to the center of your self. They can empathize with

---

[3] *The Standard Edition,* vol. XII, p. 125.

you and perhaps console you, but your situation will remain unchanged. And no matter how close you are to your friends, you will eventually be reluctant to discuss with them your innermost secrets. You can do this freely with your therapist. No judgment or surprise will be voiced by your therapist, no matter what you say.

In selecting an analyst much depends on your ability to pay his fee and to maintain such payments for a long period of time. If you have a limited income and no savings, your best course of action is to get in touch with one of the many referral services found in the larger cities. Usually, you will be able to obtain a therapist at fees ranging from $10 to $20 per visit. You should be aware that most of these therapists are at the beginning of building up a practice, but that does not necessarily mean that they are not fine therapists. The main training institutes provide low-cost therapy by their interns, and some of the larger hospitals maintain an outpatient clinic where some kind of low-fee therapy is offered.

If you seek a therapist or analyst on a private basis you will discover that their fees range anywhere from $25 to $75, depending on many factors. Many M.D. analysts charge from $40 to $50, while some of the Ph.D. therapists still charge $25 to $35. Then, too, the fact that the analyst is well known for his publications and general standing in the field might be justification for a relatively high fee. In a later chapter I will discuss some of the reasons why analysts have to charge the high fees they do.

It should be clear that unless you are prepared to

put up the money and even to sacrifice some of the luxuries of your day-to-day living, it is a waste of time and money even to start psychoanalysis. Many patients embark on an analysis and then after a while decide that they no longer want to spend the money. In doing so they have wasted their money and the therapist's valuable time.

You should understand that if you are entering psychoanalysis, as contrasted to psychotherapy, you will be expected to see your analyst at least three times a week, a schedule that is necessary for any kind of depth therapy, regardless of the school of psychoanalysis. Some analysts will require four or even five visits a week. Many other therapists nowadays see their patients in what they call psychoanalytically oriented psychotherapy, and feel that two visits a week is sufficient.

When you are in psychotherapy proper, that is, a more supportive or directive therapy, you will be seen only once a week. Again, let me point out that this does not mean that you are in analysis. Nor should you expect the classic pattern of psychoanalysis to manifest itself in your once-a-week therapy. Some therapists even put patients on the couch, which is sheer nonsense since the couch is part of the in-depth treatment that cannot possibly take place in psychotherapy.

In selecting your therapist, you must realize how important his personality is. You should expect to deal with a man who is relaxed and alert with his patients and is himself relatively free of severe neuroses and personality problems. He should be *intact,* and not project any residues of his own neuroses. Above all, you should be able to count on his integrity.

Your analyst should be *therapeutic* in the sense that he is primarily concerned with getting you in better shape. Unfortunately, some of the recent therapies have stressed involvement of the therapist to the extent that he himself brings his own problems and unresolved neuroses to the analytic situation. Involvement of the therapist with the patient is only justified if it is in the interest of the patient. All other involvements are rationalizations on the therapist's part for involving himself neurotically and often destructively with the patient.

Involvement of the therapist's personality *can* be helpful if, for instance, the therapist were to cite personal experiences that might prove to be helpful and enlightening to his patient, but the patient's welfare should be foremost.

The question of sleeping with one's analyst (discussed in greater detail in Chapter IV) has become quite a topic of discussion among both analysts and patients. In my opinion an analyst who sleeps with his patient is a testimony to his own unresolved sexual problems and a poor personal analysis. Pity those analysts who might have to recruit their sexual partners from their patient population. They have taken advantage of an enormously delicate transference situation that exists between patient and analyst, and in doing so they are no longer capable and responsible analysts. They forget that the patient presenting himself for treatment did not come for the purpose of sleeping with his analyst but to be helped and to be cured.

Many analysts with too narcissistic an ego love the adulation of their patients and then in a foolish way believe that their patients' *transference* feelings are real feelings toward them. When Freud writes of the "fire of transference-love" he undoubtedly also had in mind the analyst's countertransference feelings. It is also quite well known that Freud considered the analyst's countertransference one of the most crucial and decisive issues in the analytic situation. As a matter of fact, he recognized that on various occasions he had encountered serious difficulties with his countertransference. There is a beautiful example of Freud's countertransference with one of his famous patients, Hilda Doolittle. When Freud saw H.D. in analysis he was already in his late seventies and must have had strong feelings about his attraction to her. In an emotional outburst during one of her analytic sessions, he declares: "The trouble is—I am an old man—*you do not think it worth your while to love me.*"[4] Needless to say, H.D. was rather puzzled by this statement.

With the onset of the new therapies both radical and encounter, the role of the therapist has been blurred. Whereas the analyst's detachment in many analytic situations is *beneficial* to the patient, it is now considered almost in bad taste for an analyst to maintain some semblance of analytic neutrality. Many patients do not realize that detachment and neutrality do not necessarily mean that the analyst is not a warm and open person. On the contrary, the wise analyst

[4] H.D., *Tribute to Freud* (New York: Pantheon Books, 1956), p. 21.

will know when and how to show his concern for the patient he is treating.

Present-day analysts who embrace their patients at the drop of a hat and engage in all kinds of physical activities with them are not necessarily wise and strategic analysts. They often do not know the essentials of analytic and therapeutic treatment, and only act that way because they themselves are afraid of the discipline of the analytic situation and process.

But now you finally have selected your analyst and you are ready to present yourself for your first interview. You may be tempted to cancel your appointment and you are filled with anxiety about the impending meeting. In the next chapter I will discuss some of the implications of that initial interview, both for the patient and for the analyst.

Chapter 2

WHAT DO I NEED?

You have made your telephone call and you have heard his voice. Now you are prepared to meet the analyst for your first interview. You might have wanted to ask him questions on the phone. Most of the time during this first telephone call an analyst will confine himself to asking you only who referred you to him. You might then ask what his fees are. Some analysts will tell you their fee over the phone. Others prefer to discuss this with you during the first interview. Some have a standard charge for the initial consultation, but that charge may differ from their regular fee. Some may not even charge you for the initial interview, although those analysts are so few as to represent an endangered species.

You arrive at the analyst's office and right away you begin to have various reactions. He may have his office in his home, which often means that the office will reveal something of his personality or of his personal life, whereas those therapists who see patients outside their homes often have offices that reflict a certain impersonality or even sterility. Your reactions to the office may be so strong that you will want to express them as soon as you enter. Remember not to suppress anything you might want to say. Your prospective analyst is prepared for your comments.

Don't think that you will insult him if you tell him that you don't care for his taste in office furniture or decoration. Your every reaction during the initial interview is important.

Most analysts will let you start by telling them about your reason for making an appointment. If you are at a loss for words or if you feel inhibited, some analysts will encourage you to talk by asking you questions. Others will adhere strictly to their nondirective position and will not ask you any questions.

Regardless of the school to which your therapist belongs, this is still a very valid rule for starting the analysis. The uniqueness of the therapeutic situation is that you are *free* to bring up anything you want to. Again, Freud:

One more thing before you start. What you tell me must differ in one respect from an ordinary conversation. Ordinarily you rightly keep a connecting thread running through your remarks and you exclude any intrusive ideas that may occur to you and any side-issues, so as not to wander too far from the point. But in this case you must proceed differently. You will notice that as you relate things various thoughts will occur to you which you would like to put aside on the ground of certain criticism and objections. You will be tempted to say to yourself that this or that is irrelevant here, or is quite unimportant, or nonsensical, so that there is no need to say it. You must never give in to these criticisms, but you must say it in spite of them—indeed, you must say it precisely *because* you feel an aversion to doing so. Later on you will find out and learn to understand the reason for this injunction, which is really the only one you have to follow. So say whatever goes through your mind. Act as though, for instance, you were a traveller sitting next to the window of a railway carriage and describing to someone inside the carriage the changing views which you see outside. Finally, never forget that you have promised to be absolutely honest, and never leave anything out because, for some reason or other, it is unpleasant to tell it.[1]

Do not forget that the above quotation from Freud still stands as one of the most fundamental rules for beginning the treatment. You are not just going for a chat with your family doctor; you are, hopefully, going to make one of the most important commitments in your life.

Your initial feelings about your prospective analyst are enormously important. It does not serve any purpose to start therapy or analysis with a man whom you initially do not like. It is altogether different when negative feelings about your analyst come up later in the treatment situation. Then you will have to face and confront those feelings, express them, and work them through with his help.

Do not hesitate to ask your prospective therapist questions about his background and training. As I have already indicated, you are entitled to know that he has a sound professional background. You will

[1] Freud, "On Beginning the Treatment," *Standard Edition,* vol. XII, p. 134.

find that questions concerning his personal life are not always answered. Most analysts believe that it is your personal life that is at issue and that should be the main focus of discussion; they think it is inappropriate to discuss themselves.

You will likely discover during the initial interview whether your future therapist is more directive or non-directive. You will have to decide how you feel about that. Some analysts try to make their patients feel at ease by being somewhat chatty during the first interview. Others feel that they should remain relatively neutral. You might decide that the prospective analyst is too silent for your taste, but that does not always determine whether or not he is a good therapist. One of the main functions of the analyst is *to listen* and allow his patient to express himself as much as he wants to.

This consistency is also reflected in the matter of time, which Freud stressed very heavily in his discussion of the beginning of the analytic treatment. Many analysts have found themselves in constant trouble with their schedule because they allowed their patients to cancel an appointment on twenty-four hours' notice. Consequently they will find themselves with empty hours. Patients should realize that therapists are not general practitioners or dentists, who have far more leeway as a result of the much larger number of patients they see.

Freud writes this about time:

In regard to time, I adhere strictly to the principle of leasing a definite hour. Each patient is allotted a particular hour of my available working day; it belongs to him and he is liable for it, even if he does not make use of it. This arrangement, which is taken as a matter of course for teachers of music or languages in good society, may perhaps seem too rigorous in a doctor, or even unworthy of his profession. There will be an inclination to point to the many accidents which may prevent the patient from attending every day at the same hour and it will be expected that some allowance shall be made for the numerous intercurrent ailments which may occur in the course of a longish analytic treatment. But my answer is: no other way is practicable. Under a less stringent regime the "occasional" non-attendances increase so greatly that the doctor finds his material existence threatened; whereas when the arrangement is adhered to, it turns out that accidental hindrances do not occur at all and intercurrent illnesses only very seldom. The analyst is hardly ever put in the position of enjoying a leisure hour which he is paid for and would be ashamed of; and he can continue his work without interruptions, and is spared the distressing and bewildering experience of finding that a break for which he cannot blame himself is always bound to happen just when the work promises to be especially important and rich in content.[2]

Many patients object to this approach, but, as Freud stated quite clearly, no other way is practicable. The

[2] Freud, "On Beginning the Treatment," pp. 126–27.

consistency of the treatment is at stake and you, the patient, should realize that the therapist is the main consistent fact in the analysis and that he is going to be there regardless of whether the patient comes or not.

Another important point that must be decided in the first interview is the question of the fee. Most therapists, as already noted, have standard fees. Some, however, will adjust their fee to the income of the patient. You should realize that all matters concerning money in the therapy have to be *consistent*. If not, the patient is presented with an opportunity to act out against the therapist.

Most therapists prefer that no actual money be exchanged during the course of the session and will ask that you send a check every month. A therapist will usually insist that his patients follow a consistent procedure of paying him, and he will not let them run up large bills. Naturally, he will make exceptions with patients who face unexpected financial difficulties beyond their control. But it is not beneficial for the therapeutic process if a patient owes substantial sums, since he will likely feel guilty about it and this will inhibit him from expressing himself freely in the session. The patient may, for example, feel that he cannot get angry at the therapist because he owes him money and the therapist for his part might feel, "He has some nerve, acting out at me. After all, he owes me all that money!"

Freud considered the question of the fee as another topic of the utmost importance to be discussed in the first interview.

An analyst does not dispute that money is to be regarded in the first instance as a medium for self-preservation and for obtaining power; but he maintains that, besides this, powerful sexual factors are involved in the value set upon it. He can point out that money matters are treated by civilized people in the same way as sexual matters —with the same inconsistency, prudishness and hypocrisy. The analyst is therefore determined from the first not to fall in with this attitude, but, in his dealings with his patients, to treat of money matters with the same matter-of-course frankness to which he wishes to educate them in things relating to sexual life. He shows them that he himself has cast off false shame on these topics, by voluntarily telling them the price at which he values his time. Ordinary good sense cautions him, furthermore, not to allow large sums of money to accumulate, but to ask for payment at fairly short regular intervals—monthly, perhaps. (It is a familiar fact that the value of the treatment is not enhanced in the patient's eyes if a very low fee is asked.)[3]

A number of the early analysts besides Sándor Ferenczi, the generally acknowledged pioneer of "active therapy" whom Freud on various occasions called "my son," were "actively" inclined in their therapeutic techniques. Anaïs Nin has also provided us with an intimate portrait of Otto Rank as an active and aware analyst. She writes:

---

[3] Freud, "On Beginning the Treatment," p. 131.

Dr. Rank has an agile, leaping quality of mind. I see him always as the man with very open eyes and I hear his favorite phrase which he repeats with elation: "You see? You see, eh?" And there is much more, there is always more. He is inexhaustible. When he shrugs his shoulders, then I know that he has dismissed the unessential. He has a sense of the essential, the vital. His mind is always focused. His understanding never wavers. Expansion. A joyous fertility of ideas. The gift for elevating incident into destiny.[4]

The importance of your therapist's experience, personality, sense of self, his ability to relate and yet to maintain a certain detachment cannot be stressed enough. You should understand that a great deal is required of him. Because of the *unique* and tremendously private relationship he has with you, he is essentially a lonely person. Many of the things you share with him he must keep to himself. To be able to do this, much is required in terms of character and intactness of personality.

Harry Stack Sullivan, perhaps one of America's most outstanding and brilliant psychoanalysts, saw the role of the therapist as a *participant observer*. He placed a great deal of emphasis on the therapist's own personal experiences, the proscriptions of culture so to speak:

The facts are that we cannot make any sense of the motor movements of another person except on

---

[4] *The Diary of Anaïs Nin* (New York: Harcourt, Brace & World, 1966), vol. I, p. 295.

the basis of meaningful behavior that we have experienced or seen done under circumstances in which its purpose, or at least the intentions behind it, were communicated to us. The therapist has an inescapable involvement in all that goes on in the interview; and to the extent that he is unconscious or unwitting of his participation in the interview, to that extent he does not know what is happening.[5]

Of course, Dr. Sullivan was an extremely experienced and able therapist and one who was even capable of seeing patients in analysis who were considered the least accessible to psychoanalytic treatment. Sullivan stressed also that the patient must feel that the analyst is capable and expert:

The interview is set up as an expert-client relationship, and the patient must experience something that impresses him as really expert capacity for handling him. When it comes to what you think of as "expert handling," if you will pause to consider the people whom you look upon as "understanding," that is, able to handle you expertly, you will pause to consider the people whom you look upon as "understanding," that is, able to handle you expertly, you will notice that there is demonstrated by them a very considerable show of respect for you. Meeting such a person can be a really significant event; it is almost a

[5] See Mary Julian White, "Sullivan and Treatment" in *The Contributions of Harry Stack Sullivan*, Patrick Mullahy, ed. (New York: Hermitage House, 1952), p. 121.

privilege to have him around. You are well managed primarily when you are treated as worth the trouble, and secondarily when the person is keenly aware of disturbances in your feeling of personal worth while in his presence, in other words, disturbances in your security. When he sees that a certain question is going to touch on a topic which will make you feel insecure or anxious, he makes a little preliminary movement which assures you that he is quite aware of the unpleasantness that will attend this question, but that also it is obviously necessary that he should know the information; in other words, he gives you a little warning to brace yourself. Now and then he recognizes that you are having emotions, and possibly anxiety about something which to the doctor seems to be among the most natural things on earth; and at that time he perhaps comes in and says, "Well, do you feel that that's unusual?" or something like that; and you say, "Well, yes, doctor, I'm afraid I do," and he says, "Dear me, why, I never heard anybody talk honestly who didn't mention that," and so on.[6]

You may discover that your therapist is not saying very much at all during the first session nor for that matter during quite a number of sessions. He may belong to the school that believes that, especially at the beginning of treatment, the therapist should play a passive but attentive role. In that kind of approach activity is virtually excluded, and you will begin to

[6] White, "Sullivan and Treatment," pp. 122–123.

wonder how long he will let you go on "rambling" like that. However, with his silence, he is representing a major philosophical trend in psychoanalysis which believes that in the early stages of the analysis the patient should be given every opportunity to express himself. Hence a therapist of this school will not give you startling revelations and he will keep his interpretations at a minimum if he gives them at all.

Don't think that such an analyst is lazy or is just taking it easy. He is very much there and well aware of what is going on in the analytic situation. While he listens he is planning his strategy and will slowly move in when he feels that you are ready for his interpretations.

Since so many new forms of therapy have emerged in the last decade and there has been a corresponding increase of unqualified and inadequately trained therapists, it is imperative that you take great care in selecting your therapist. You might, for example, be interested in a Gestalt therapist or an encounter therapist, both of whom are relatively new on the scene. It is entirely legitimate for you to ask such therapists where they were trained and what their general philosophy of therapy is. Since such analysts are not traditional analysts they will not interpret your question as initial resistance but will answer your questions quite honestly.

In the end you have to realize that while you may have checked out an analyst's credentials thoroughly and found them totally satisfactory, the most important consideration for you is: "How do I feel about him? Am I comfortable with him?" A sense of initial trust is fundamental for the pursuit of your treatment. Once that is established you can move on and you can begin to ask yourself the questions I will discuss in the next chapter.

Chapter 3

WHAT CAN YOU DO FOR ME?

You might come to your therapy with great expectations. You may have heard from your friends that spectacular things happen during therapy and you are obviously eager to experience them. But brace yourself; your expectations are not going to be fulfilled immediately or even in a slightly longer time. Although you may experience changes in your life situation at the beginning of your therapy, do not consider such changes as permanent. They are often a result of your positive feeling for your analyst and they do not mean that you have touched the fundamental causes of your problem.

What you may have experienced if such early changes occur is the "analytic honeymoon." In most analyses there is an initial period where the interpretations of your analyst seem to be virtually changing your world. Some of the symptoms you may have complained about upon entering analysis might have disappeared, but again this does not constitute a permanent change.

What is interesting about these initial successes is their *dramatic* impact upon the patient, and his belief, and sometimes even the analyst's belief, that a cure has been achieved. Some of the pioneer analysts experienced these successes as cures and hence terminated their patients' treatment after the removal of symptoms.

The early analysts, particularly those who were active about 1910, achieved these therapeutic results with a technique closely resembling one that Freud had already abandoned ten or fifteen years before. This technique had certain characteristics which we may describe as "primitive": the analyst was very *active* and paid little or no attention either to resistance or to transference—and this at a time when Freud was already writing of transference as "inevitable" and discussing at length how it was used by the patient as resistance.[1] Not only this, but the atmosphere and subject matter of the analyses also had certain primitive characteristics: the analytic situation was extremely *dramatic* and often culminated in the confession of some traumatic sexual experience. All these primitive characteristics gradually disappeared after 1914, however.

The successes of the early analysts have been the subject of a great deal of speculation. Dr. Michael Balint, a student of Sándor Ferenczi, who himself experimented with an "active" technique, feels that these early successes should be attributed to the therapist's enthusiasm. Perhaps the intense interest of any worker new to this field engenders a correspondingly heightened excitement in the patient,* with the result that repressed feelings come easily to the surface and are

[1] Sigmund Freud, "The Dynamics of Transference," *Standard Edition,* vol. XII.

* Supervising analysts who have young therapists in training will confirm this. Patients of young therapists often are *carried* by the enthusiasm of their therapist.

experienced with such intensity and completeness that no further working through is thought to be necessary. This excitement can never quite be recaptured subsequently, nor can its effects. This may partly account for the prevalence in the early analytic material of traumatic experiences—those moments in our lives in which so many feelings, already present, are suddenly concentrated and crystallized by some external circumstance.

When you walk in for your first regular session with your therapist one of your earliest questions might well be "Shall I sit up?" or "Shall I lie down on the couch?" You should understand that analysts have a variety of approaches to this subject. Most of them believe that if you are entering depth analysis, involving visits three or four times a week, you should lie down and be able to regress in the service of the ego. Freud himself had somewhat mixed thoughts about the subject:

> I must say a word about a certain ceremonial which concerns the position in which the treatment is carried out. I hold to the plan of getting the patient to lie on a sofa while I sit behind him out of his sight. This arrangement has a historical basis; it is the remnant of the hypnotic method out of which psycho-analysis was evolved. But it deserves to be maintained for many reasons. The first is a personal motive, but one which others may share with me. I cannot put up with being stared at by other people for eight hours a day (or more). Since, while I am listening to the pa-

tient, I, too, give myself over to the current of my unconscious thoughts, I do not wish my expressions of face to give the patient material for interpretations or to influence him in what he tells me. The patient usually regards being made to adopt this position as a hardship and rebels against it, especially if the instinct for looking (scopophilia) plays an important part in his neurosis. I insist on this procedure, however, for its purpose and result are to prevent the transference from mingling with the patient's associations imperceptibly, to isolate the transference and to allow it to come forward in due course sharply defined as a resistance. I know that many analysts work in a different way, but I do not know whether this deviation is due more to a craving for doing things differently or to some advantage which they find they gain by it.[2]

So you see that Freud considered both his own and the patient's interests in this matter. When your analyst is involved and active he will probably ask you to sit up, or he may let you make the choice.

It might also be interesting to observe here that not only Freud thought it better that patients lie down, but that Medard Boss, one of the best-known existential analysts, defended the rule that the patient should lie down during treatment. However, he defends it for other reasons:

---

[2] Sigmund Freud, "On Beginning the Treatment," *Standard Edition*, vol. XII, pp. 133–34.

Freud's insistence on the patient's reclining—making it impossible for him to see the therapist—reveals his deep, though unarticulated, awareness of man's basic condition, as Daseinsanalysis* has brought it to light, regardless of the seemingly extraneous reasons he gave for this rule. For to let the patient lie down in the analytic situation takes cognizance of the human body itself as a sphere of human existence; it is not merely an apparatus or an organism attached in some enigmatic way to a psyche. For this reason an analysand does not comply fully with the demand to let himself become aware of all his characteristics without censoring them beforehand (as being of higher or lower value) unless he loosens up physically, too, while lying horizontally, so that all his limbs are also on the same level. The conventional arrangement in which physician and patient sit facing each other corresponds—as far as the respective bodily spheres of their existences are concerned—to the traditional conception of two subjects, separate and standing opposite each other. Thus the physical juxtaposition implicitly preserves the conceptions of rank and value systems which the patient brings into the therapeutic situation. Sitting opposite the therapist enforces the patient's tendency to resist the basic rule of psychoanalytic therapy, by leaving "above" (in the widest sense) what has always been "above," and leaving "below" what always was "below." Furthermore, erect stature is the position *par*

* Daseinsanalysis is equivalent to existential analysis.

excellence of self-assertion. It accentuates self-glorification, as much as the supremacy of everything that belongs to the head, the elevation of the spirit (the higher and the lighter) raised *above* the lower and sensual pole (base, animalistic, abysmal).[3]

You should know that many contemporary therapists would not agree with either Freud or Boss on this issue. They maintain that the dialogue between therapist and patient, which they view as essential to the therapeutic situation, cannot take place when the patient lies on a couch. They also feel that therapists who sit behind their patients largely remove themselves from the therapeutic situation as well as from the patient.

Many patients have strong feelings about lying down, and feel that they cannot communicate sufficiently with their therapists if they lie down. In the end, whether you lie down or sit up during therapy is your decision. After all, if you feel uncomfortable in lying down you must communicate this fact to your therapist. Remember that holding back feelings is detrimental to your therapy. You have to express all that you feel, and that applies from the very beginning of your therapy—everything that happens as soon as you have entered the therapist's office for the first time.

When your analyst does not ask questions and in a sense "lets you just sit (or lie) there," it is not be-

[3] Medard Boss, *Psychoanalysis and Daseinsanalysis* (New York: Basic Books, 1963), pp. 62–63.

cause he is lazy, but because you are *resisting*. In any kind of therapeutic situation, it is important for you to recognize that you have to provide the material, in other words, to produce the necessary elements with which the therapist can work. Do not think it is easy for a therapist to sit and be silent. He is very much there with you, and will try to pick up other signs of your being there, such as facial expressions, the way you sit in the chair, or even in the way you lie on the couch. Any sign, nonverbal though it may be, is an important indication to the therapist of what is going on with you.

Then again, when you enter your earliest sessions you might even talk too much. As Ferenczi once remarked, "With several patients talkativeness proved to be a method of resistance. They discussed all conceivable immaterial matters superficially in order not to have to speak or reflect on a few important ones."[4]

How much the analyst talks and when will depend on the kind of analyst you have. An existential analyst, for example, might describe for you or define your particular *limited* world design. He does not feel that he is necessarily breaking psychoanalytic rules by talking himself rather than letting you do the talking. Medard Boss defines the attitude of the existential analyst toward his patient in the following way:

He can devote himself fully to the analysand in the "evenly-hovering attention" that Freud

---

[4] Sándor Ferenczi, *Further Contributions to the Theory and Technique of Psychoanalysis* (New York: Basic Books, 1960), p. 252.

always demanded. He does not approach the patient from the point of view of a scientific theory nor is his attention distracted by the observation of assumed anonymous forces within the patient. Instead, the analyst's behavior rests on the insight that, being human, he is called upon to disclose both things and men. This knowledge increases his sensitivity to all the obstacles which generally reduce the potential relationships of a patient to a few rigid and unauthentic modes of behavior. Such sensitivity in turn enables the Daseinsanalyst to carry out an "analysis of resistance," wherein the patient is tirelessly confronted with the limitations of his life and wherein these limitations are incessantly questioned, so that the possibility of a richer existence is implied. As a rule, neurotically reduced people regard their wretched interpersonal relations as the only ones possible. They do not know that greater freedom is available. If their restrictions are repeatedly questioned, previously non-admitted possibilities of behavior regularly appear, along with perception of the things and fellow human beings who belong to these world-disclosing possibilities.[5]

In later visits to your therapist you will probably discover that he is not always the same. Not only does he have his moods, too, but you should also consider that the analytic process cannot be unvarying. You—and of course your analyst—are the only consistent factors in the process. But he might change

---

[5] Boss, *Psychoanalysis and Daseinsanalysis*, p. 234.

his mind about certain strategies in the analytic situation.

An active analyst, for example, might not always be active. Mary Julian White in writing about Sullivan as an analyst says:

Activity was not manifested by Sullivan every hour. There might be long periods of work with little intervention. He taught this also, as follows: "If a patient is talking and you don't quite know what he is talking about, and yet at the end of an hour you have a sense that he is getting somewhere, leave him alone. But if you have no sense that he is getting somewhere, you may say, "Somehow I don't believe that I follow today—I can't see where we've gone—perhaps you can make it clearer next time."[6]

Realize that not only will your therapist be observing you, but that you to quite the same extent will be observing him. You will look for verbal and nonverbal signs from him about how your therapy is going. As one patient of Sullivan described it:

I would suddenly become aware of a change in him, like the alertness of a pointer who has spotted a bird. It was a certain wave of thoughtful, kindly alertness, totally non-verbal. That knowledge of his already being where I didn't

---

[6] Mary Julian White, "Sullivan and Treatment" in *The Contributions of Harry Stack Sullivan*, Patrick Mullahy, ed. (New York: Hermitage House, 1952), p. 130.

know where I was going, made it possible for me successfully to go through a number of rough spots.[7]

Often you will ask your therapist if he knows where you are going or whether he now knows all about you. Much of the material you have brought to the initial sessions may have helped him to recognize your life designs and may also have given him a clue as to what patterns the analysis will take on and approximately what your role is going to be in that process. The fact that the analyst has a pretty good picture of what you are about does not mean that you are going to be helped in two or three sessions. It is *you* who will have to arrive at the insights which will enable you to deal better with your problems.

In terms of the question "What can he do for me?" you should realize that the analyst *already* is doing something for you simply by being there with you in the analytic situation. Analysts on the whole do not give specific advice. In the analytic situation the insight has to come from you. He is there *literally* to *analyze* your life situation and not to give you specific directions. Yes, in an existential analysis the analyst might at a certain point, after you have been in analysis for some time, present you with a number of alternatives and choices regarding your life situation. But it is up to you to *choose* or *make your decision*. The opportunity to do so is all yours, and only then can it be productive and fruitful for you. That is not

---

[7] White, "Sullivan and Treatment," p. 132.

to say that a therapist might not use certain techniques to shake you up and to get you moving. Ferenczi reports that many patients in his care improved considerably after he "shook them up," provided he adhered to the following rules:

> First of all, we never promise the patient that he will be cured by the attempt; on the contrary, we prepare him for the eventual worsening of his subjective condition immediately after the attempt. We only say to him—and that justifiably—that *in ultima analysi* the attempt will prove helpful in the treatment.
>
> Secondly, we renounce thereby all the otherwise usual means of forcible or coaxing suggestion, and leave it to the patient whether he will decide to make this attempt. He must already have a fairly good degree of psychoanalytic insight into the treatment if he carries out our request.[8]

In asking what your analyst can do for you, you should compare entering analysis to a long journey in which you are going to have a fellow passenger-guide along the way. He will keep you company and he will point out the sights to you, but you must decide where to travel and what your impressions of the journey's highlights are.

You will recognize your therapist's orientation by the way he responds to the material you provide. The

8 Ferenczi, *Further Contributions to the Theory and Technique of Psychoanalysis*, p. 237.

comparison between the traditional psychoanalyst and the existentially oriented analyst is extremely pertinent here. Boss writes:

> The Daseinsanalyst often asks his patients, "Why not?" thereby encouraging them to even greater tests of daring. "Why is it you don't dare to behave in such-and-such a manner during the analytic session?" is a question which is often asked in place of the usual analytic "Why?" If the "Why?" comes too early, before the analysand has had sufficient time for acting out, it puts too great demands on him and may worsen his condition instead of improving it. Most patients are caught in a mechanistic, causal-genetic interpretation of themselves. If we ask "Why?" prematurely, they will in most cases understand this to mean that they should look for the cause of their present behavior in an earlier period of their lives. At the same time, we may awaken false hopes in them. They may get the impression that simply finding the presumed cause of suffering (an event in early childhood which "fixated libido" at a specific level of development) will remove the obstacles against getting well. But in the strict sense of the term, no event in the life history of a person can ever be the "cause" of neurotic symptoms.[9]

Many roads lead to Rome and there are equally as many approaches to psychotherapy that can be beneficial to you and others.

---

[9] Boss, *Psychoanalysis and Daseinsanalysis,* p. 248.

In the course of your analysis you might find that everything that happens in it is not always pleasant, or you may discover that there are long periods when you seem to be standing still. Often at such a time your analyst will give you some reassurance that things are still moving along. Here again Sullivan comes to mind:

At times, Dr. Sullivan would give reassurance when a patient seemed to be mulling along without apparent progress. He described his way of handling this as follows: "I say quite simply that I have definitely a feeling that something is in progress, that I cannot guess what, and I can quite understand the patient's feeling puzzled, but I suggest that we struggle along as is for the time being. That's all the patient needs. If he has received the assurance that this is not a hopelessly befogged area, he will plug along somewhat better. Before very long something usually appears which one can see in retrospect required a lot of preparation, so that concepts rather remote and quite thoroughly misunderstood by the patient could finally be communicated; whereupon I beam and say, 'Well, don't I hear you saying so-and-so?'—and the patient says, 'Good God, I think so.' Then I remember that this has been a hard pull, and I say, 'Well, perhaps we are now getting the returns on this very obscure effort. Let's go right ahead now, and we may even come to see why the effort itself was necessary.' "[10]

---

[10] Patrick Mullahy (ed.), *The Contributions of Harry Stack Sullivan* (New York: Hermitage House, 1952), pp. 133–34.

In the end you have to ask yourself the question "How much of this can I take?" Much has been written about how strong or weak a patient's ego should be in order to endure, if you will, the analytic process. Usually analysts prefer, at least in analytic treatment, patients whose egos are fairly intact. Patients with fragile egos have a more difficult time working through an analytic process. Especially when you are in depth analysis and you visit your analyst several times a week, you are bound to experience a great deal of pressure at given times, and your analyst will have to decide whether you are strong enough to take it. If he is a good diagnostician he will have satisfied himself that your particular mental situation will be sufficiently strong to take whatever comes your way in the analytic process. If your ego is too fragile he will then have advised you not to undertake a depth analysis but simply enter psychotherapy and come to his office once or twice a week. If he decides to do just that he will have done so in your own interest and he will then explore other methods of helping you cope with your problems in a therapeutic situation.

Responsible analysts and therapists will explore all possible alternatives with you so that you may find the right kind of therapeutic treatment for your particular problems. Your own ability to pursue the analytic process in its many aspects is one of the determining factors for the analyst in deciding what kind of therapeutic treatment you need.

But by now you have gone through your first analytic sessions and you are gradually wondering what is happening to you. Moreover, you are beginning to become aware of certain feelings for your analyst. These feelings probably seem puzzling, but you have now come up against one of the most important aspects of analytic treatment: the transference situation, or "What do I feel about my analyst?"

Chapter 4

TALKING TO YOUR THERAPIST: FREE ASSOCIATION AND DREAMS

Your contribution to the therapeutic process is mainly verbal. In plain language: *Talk!* Yes, silence can sometimes be very fruitful in the therapeutic process,[1] but on the whole your talking is what furthers it. And as I have stated previously, you should talk about anything that comes to your mind.

As I also noted earlier, whether the therapist does or does not push you into talking depends on him and his particular orientation. The orthodox therapist will not start with questioning you. He will wait until you produce the material; in other words, you have to start talking. He will not introduce any material that is *not yours*. After you begin to talk he might question you, but not before. A more active therapist will intervene and encourage you to talk. He will break your silence and probably present you with his interpretation of it. In that kind of therapy the dialogue in a sense has replaced the one-sided participation of the patient in classical analysis.

But, again, don't forget that *any repression* of ma-

---

[1] See M. Masud R. Khan, "Silence As Communication," *Bulletin of the Menninger Clinic,* vol. 27, no. 6, November, 1963), pp. 300–317. Also in Hendrik M. Ruitenbeek (ed.), *The Analytic Situation* (Chicago: Aldine-Atherton, 1973).

terial only hurts you and the therapy. It necessarily slows down the therapeutic process, and in the end you will only have to work harder in order to reveal the repressed material.

In most analyses the discussion of dream material is highly important. In shorter analyses and in supportive therapy less emphasis is placed on dream material. Freud, of course, believed that the discussion of dream material was the cornerstone of psychoanalysis. In fact, in the days when patients visited their analysts five days a week, the analysis became very much a dream analysis. The patient would bring his dreams to the analyst every twenty-four hours so that some kind of a continuum was established.

There are a few basic rules that govern the discussion of dreams in *any* kind of analysis. Under no circumstance should you discuss your dreams with someone other than the analyst. Your analyst must be the first to hear the dream. If you break this rule the dream becomes worthless in terms of analysis, because you have already distorted it to a great extent. The longer the time between the dream and its presentation in the analytic situation the greater the possibility of distortion. So don't discuss your dreams during the morning coffee break prior to your lunch-hour analytic session.

If you have had several dreams preceding an analytic session your analyst should not let you relate them all at once, because there might not be enough time left to discuss any of them. You will simply have taken up the whole of your analytic session that day *by relating* your dreams and *not associating* to them. Incidentally, patients who recount very long dreams are usually thought to be resisting, because here, too, the result of narrating a dream might mean there would not be enough time left in your session to discuss it.

If you have any dreams at all you should bring them up at the beginning of the session. You and the analyst will then have the opportunity to examine them. If a patient tries to relate a dream at the close of a session ("Oh, yes, I had this important dream last night!"), the analyst will interpret this as resistance, because the simple fact that you brought the dream up at the end of the session indicates that you do not want to discuss it at all.

A longtime controversy in psychoanalysis is the question of whether analysts should allow their patients to write down their dreams.[2] When you visit your analyst only once or twice a week you probably should write down your dreams. When you see your analyst three or more times a week it would be better not to do so. Writing down the dream distorts it, even at the very moment that you are writing it.

There will be times when you cannot produce a dream. Don't worry too much about that. Enough other material is available for the analyst to interpret. As Freud stated:

One must in general guard against displaying very special interest in the interpretation of dreams, or arousing an idea in the patient that

---

[2] Karl Abraham, "Should Patients Write Down Their Dreams," in Karl Abraham, *Clinical Papers and Essays on Psychoanalysis* (New York: Basic Books, 1955), pp. 33–35.

the work would come to a standstill if he were
to bring up no dreams; otherwise there is a danger of the resistance being *directed* (emphasis
added, H.M.R.) to the production of dreams, with
a consequent cessation of them. The patient
must be brought to believe, on the contrary, that
the analysis invariably finds material for its con-
tinuation, regardless of whether or not he brings
up dreams or what amount of attention is devoted
to them.[3]

Your analyst will not always interpret every dream
you bring to the analysis. As a matter of strategy he
might decide not to deal with your dream. He also
might feel that your dream will be produced again.
Dreams, or at least their content, repeat themselves.
In this regard Freud stated:

We have found from fine examples of fully ana-
lysed dreams that several successive scenes of
one dream may have the same content, which
may find expression in them with increasing clar-
ity; and we have learnt, too, that several dreams
occurring in the same night need be nothing more
than attempts, expressed in various forms, to
represent one meaning. In general, we may rest
assured that every wishful impulse which creates
a dream today will re-appear in other dreams as
long as it has not been understood and withdrawn
from the domination of the unconscious. It often

[3] Sigmund Freud, "The Handling of Dream-Interpretation," *Standard
Edition*, vol. XII, pp. 92–93.

happens, therefore, that the best way to complete the interpretation of a dream is to leave it and to devote one's attention to a new dream, which may contain the same material in a possibly more accessible form.[4]

The main objective of the analyst in analyzing and interpreting your dream is to place the content of the dream in the context of your life situation be it past or present. There are many approaches to dream interpretation. The traditional analyst is interested in getting the *latent* content of your dream as contrasted to its *manifest* content, that is, the actual sensation of the dream by you in the analytic situation. The question is: How does he determine the latent content of your dream? Most analysts on the whole still follow the Freudian technique of dream interpretation. They will first ask you to relate the dream. They might then ask questions about your thoughts immediately after you had the dream. Or they might ask you to talk about what you did the day before you had the dream. All this assists the analyst in making *connections* between the content of your dream and your actual life situation, and with the help of your free associations will bring out the latent content of the dream.

I want to illustrate the concept of *connections* in dream interpretation with the following example cited by Medard Boss.

The patient was a physician suffering from washing and cleaning compulsions. He had gone through two

---

4 Freud, "The Handling of Dream-Interpretation," p. 94.

analyses, Freudian and Jungian, before reaching Medard Boss. For some time he had had a recurrent dream involving church steeples. In the Freudian analysis the dream had been interpreted in terms of phallic symbols, while in the Jungian analysis the dream had been approached in terms of archetypal religious symbols. The patient discussed these interpretations intelligently and at length, but his compulsive behavior, after a temporary remission, recurred and was as crippling as before. During the first months of his analysis with Boss, the patient reported a recurrent dream in which he would approach a lavatory door that he would always find locked. Boss confined himself to asking each time only why the door needed to be locked—"rattling the doorknob," as he put it. Finally the patient had a dream in which he went through the door and found himself inside a church, waist-deep in feces and being tugged by a rope from up in the bell tower, which was wrapped around his waist. The patient was suspended so tautly that he thought he would be pulled to pieces. After having this dream, he then went through a psychotic episode of four days during which Medard Boss remained by his bedside. After this episode the analysis continued, with an eventual very successful outcome.

Boss points out in his discussion of the case that the patient felt guilty because he had locked up some essential potentialities in himself. *Therefore* he had guilt feelings. If, as Boss puts it, we "forget being"— by failing to bring ourselves to our entire being, *by failing to be authentic,* by slipping into the conformist anonymity of *das Mann*—then we have in fact lost our being and to that extent we are *failures*: "If you lock up potentialities (as the patient did in his dream), you are guilty against or even *indebted* to what is given you in your origin, in your 'core.' " This is an existential condition. You are indebted and guilty—and includes all guilt feelings, which manifest themselves in a thousand and one ways. Boss's patient had locked up both the bodily and the spiritual possibilities of experience. He had previously accepted the Freudian-libido and Jungian-archetype explanations and was all too familiar with them, but that is a good way of escaping the whole thing. Because the patient did not accept and take into his existence these two possibilities, he was both guilty and indebted to himself, and that was the origin of his neurosis.

The existential analyst views being-in-the-dream-world as one of the autonomous ways of man's existence; he treats the dream behavior of the patient in exactly the same way that he treats his waking-world relationships. This means that he submits the patient's dreamed ways of behaving and perceiving to a strict analysis of resistance. The whole therapeutic focus is on questioning the assumed necessity of the barriers of anxiety, shame, and distaste that are in one way or another *restricting* the dreamer's free relationships *within* his dream world.

I want to cite a number of other dreams reported by Boss to illustrate more fully the existential approach to dream interpretation.

A man, aged twenty-eight, dreams that he is visiting the zoo in his home town, where there are especially fine, large tigers and lions. The director of the zoo joins the dreamer and proceeds to open the heavy gate of the cage; he then enters the cage and feeds the animals with very large chunks of raw meat. The animals become excited. The patient becomes increasingly terrified when he realizes that the director has left the gate open and the seemingly solid iron bars of the cage are not made of iron at all but only of ice. Because the sun had broken through the clouds when the director arrived, the fence of ice is melting rapidly. The dreamer runs away as fast as he can and awakens out of breath.

Of course this is a rather common type of dream and Freud discussed similar dreams, both in the fashion that Jung later called interpretation on the "objective" level and in a so-called subjective way. Boss feels that the only thing that he, as an existential analyst, is justified in saying about this dream experience is that something alive—presenting itself in the phenomena of the tigers and the lions—which has been safely imprisoned is now running after the dreamer, threatening to destroy him, to devour him.

In analyzing the dream Boss first asked the patient, "Must you really be so afraid of the tigers and lions? Could you not make friends with them?" The patient retorted, "You, too, I am sure, would be terrified in such a situation." Whereupon Boss replied, "The real question is, why can the essence of nature's vitality shine forth to you only through dangerous, wild animals in your dream? Perhaps it is your anxiety about this vitality which limits your existence to the admittance of vitality's dangerous and aggressive features. Of all the possible natural and vital phenomena, only lions and tigers could appear in your dream, because the nature of their particular being alone corresponds to the anxious restriction of the *Dasein*'s openness. A fearless and free man might have encountered the essence of nature's vitality in a dream of a joyful encounter with his sweetheart, in which he embraced her wholeheartedly."

The existential analyst, in this instance, remained with the immediately given phenomena of the dreamer's world. Any further interpretation in regard to the wild animals of this dream, such as a Freudian analyst might offer, would have been an unwaranted and arbitrary imposition on their genuine phenomenological meaning. Freudian "subjective" dream interpretation would probably say that the dreamer's drives and "animal" instincts were projected onto a hallucinatory external world and were experienced as external perceptions.

Actually most traditional analysts would view this dream as a clear-cut "transference" dream, especially if they were informed, as Boss stated, that the zoo director physically resembled the analyst. Boss maintains that nothing whatever justified declaring that the zoo director actually "means" or "signifies" the doctor. The zoo director, according to Boss, refers to the analyst only insofar as the dreamer's existence had already opened up to some extent through the liberating influence of the analyst-analysand relationship. This greater openness of the patient's existence makes possible the appearance of the zoo director; the appearance of the director indicates the dreamer's awareness of the possibility of a fearless, free relationship with even the most vital phenomena of the world. Simply to see another man's fearless relationship with wild animals is of course a long way from being open to the extent that nature's vitality can shine forth in one's own fearless ways of handling the respective phenomena of the human world.

Boss tells of another case in which a twenty-year-old woman dreamed that she was sitting in a perambulator. She was still a small child in the dream, although the carriage had already become somewhat small for her. A young, healthy nurse, also about twenty years old, was pushing the baby carriage up a hill. The nurse asked the dreamer to get out and to walk on her own feet. The dreamer refused, kicking and screaming. The nurse took the dreamer out of the baby carriage, cut off her head and her limbs, buried the parts in the ground, and walked off. At this point the dreamer awoke in terror.

Boss feels that

to explain this dream as revealing severe masochistic tendencies would have been artificial and arbitrary. Nothing in the immediately given dream. refers to masochistic behavior. Nothing would have been gained therapeutically, either, by the analyst's attempt to point out hidden masochism. On the contrary, such an arbitrary explanation would have led to the endless juggling of theoretical conceptions and psychoanalytic formulas by which patients usually defend themselves against the greater harm being done to them by such unwarranted and destructive interpretations.

Boss, as an existential analyst, feels that the patient became aware of the unavoidable burial of her childish way of existing. In everybody's development, the child's world must die and give way to ever more adult ways of behavior. The terror that finally awakened the patient shows only too clearly, according to Boss, her attitude of panic toward growing up.

The existential analyst would use this dream therapeutically by first pointing out to the patient her terror of growing up and walking on her own two feet. Secondly he would assure her, by correcting the grave mistake in her self-interpretation—showing her that she is no longer a helpless little child. Already she has opened her existence to an understanding of mature womanliness, if only by being able to recognize a healthy nurse and to understand her as such. For this reason, the death of her child's world, according to the existential interpretation, cannot possibly mean total annihilation of her existence. Therefore, would it really be such a tragedy if her childish way of existing were to be superseded by her opening up to a wider and more mature world, including the awareness and understanding of grown-up womanliness? The understanding of this grown-up feature of human existence, which occurs in this dream in the patient's seeing and recognizing another grown-up woman *as* a healthy, adult woman, is the first step toward full appreciation of any mature relationships to her own self-being and carrying them out responsibly in her dreaming as well as her waking life.

The question of the latent content of a dream is important, as I pointed out earlier. However, Otto Rank, one of Freud's pupils, felt that we should deal more with the actual content on its face value. Rank relates the following case. The patient is a woman who had very ambivalent reactions toward the end of her analysis when the schedule of visits to the analyst had been cut down to three times a week. In the dream she saw three men whose penises had been cut off. Earlier in the analytic hour, before mentioning this dream, she made a speech expressing appreciation of the analyst (Rank), of her husband, and of her father, such as might often come at the end of analysis. This might be a castration dream (Rank), but the more important interpretation is probably that *she* was cutting the transference. *She* had cut off the penises—that is, herself—from the men on whom she was dependent. Cutting three times (three men) and its relation to the three days a week as the analyst had suggested previously is the most significant aspect of the dream.

Rank feels that in the analytic situation there is no one fundamental explanation. In the dream just described the whole conflict is concentrated in the three days. This must be pointed out because it is present material. Why should sexual symbolism be considered more important than any other, Rank asks. The patient's *reaction* to the dream is the most significant thing, not the content. A dream of castration may be more important on a nonsexual level; a dream with nonsexual content may have sexual significance. Here the question arises, according to Rank, of whether or not there is always a latent content to be considered.

One of the most radical dream interpreters of the last decades undoubtedly was Fritz Perls, who introduced a new dimension to dream interpretation. Perls shied away from traditional dream interpretation. He advocated the notion of letting the patient reexperience his dream in the therapeutic situation. In his group dream seminars, conducted at Esalen, he drove this point home over and over again. The following case is from his celebrated work *Gestalt Therapy Verbatim*:

> NORA: In my dream I was in an incomplete house and the stairs have no rails. I climb up the stairs and get very high, but they go nowhere. I know that in reality it would be awful to climb that high on these stairs. In the dream it's bad enough, but it's not that awful, and I always wonder how I could endure it.
>
> FRITZ: Okeh. Be this incomplete house, and repeat the dream again.
>
> NORA: Well, I climb the stairs and the stairs have no rails on the side.
>
> FRITZ: "I am an incomplete house, I have no . . ."
>
> NORA: "I am in an incomplete house and I'm climbing the stairs and—"
>
> FRITZ: Describe what kind of house you are.
>
> NORA: 'Well, it has a—
>
> FRITZ: *"I am—"* . .

NORA: I'm the house?

FRITZ: Yah, you're the house.

NORA: And the house is—

FRITZ: *"I am—"*

NORA: I am the house and I'm incomplete. And I have only the skeleton, the parts and hardly the floors. But the stairs are there. And I don't have the rails to protect me. And yet I do climb and—

FRITZ: No, no. You're the house. You don't climb.

NORA: Yet I'm climbed on. And then I end somewhere on the top, and it—and it leads nowhere and—

FRITZ: Say this to Nora. You're the house, and talk to Nora.

NORA: You're climbing on me and you're getting nowhere. And you might fall. Usually you fall.

FRITZ: You see? That's what I try to do—to climb on you and I get nowhere. It took a long time before you even could identify with the house. Now say the same thing to some people here, as the house. "If you try to climb on me . . ."

NORA: If you try to climb on me, you'll fall.

FRITZ: Can you tell me more what you're doing to them, if they're trying to live in you and so on? . . . (Nora sighs) Are you a comfortable house to live in?

NORA: No. I'm open and unprotected and there are winds blowing inside. (voice sinks to whisper) And if you climb on me you'll fall. And if you'll judge me . . . I'll fall.

FRITZ: You begin to experience something? What do you feel?

NORA: I want to fight you. I don't care about you. I *do*. I don't *want* to. (crying) . . . I don't want to cry and I don't want you—I don't even want you to see me cry, (cries) . . . I'm afraid of you . . . I don't want you to pity me.

FRITZ: Say this again.

NORA: I don't want you to pity me. I'm strong enough without you, too. I don't need you and —I, I *wish* I don't need you.

FRITZ: Okey, let the stairs have an encounter with the non-existent railings. "Railings, where are you to hold onto?"

NORA: Railings, I can live without you. I'm climbable. It would be nicer to have you though. It would be nicer to be complete, to have something on top of the concrete and to have nice polished rails.

FRITZ: What kind of floors have you got?

NORA: Concrete. Concrete floors, just uncovered . . .

FRITZ: Pretty tough, hmmm? With a solid foundation.

NORA: Yeah.

FRITZ: Can you tell this to the group, that you have solid foundations?

NORA: You can walk and it's safe and you could live with it if you don't mind being a little bit uncomfortable. I'm dependable.

FRITZ: So what do you need to be complete? . . .

NORA: I don't know, I—I don't *think* I need, I—I just feel I— want more.

FRITZ: Aha. How can we make the house a bit warmer?

NORA: Well, cover it, close—put windows in it; put walls, curtains, nice colors—nice warm colors.

FRITZ: Okeh, can you be all the supplement— all of what's missing, and talk to the incomplete house. I'm here to complete you, to supplement you.

NORA: I'm here to complete you. You are pretty good but you could be much better and much nicer to live in if you have me—you'd be warmer and brighter and softer—have nice colors, have maybe carpets and curtains, some soft and bright things and maybe some heating.

FRITZ: Change seats. Be the incomplete house.

NORA: Well, you're luxury. You can do without luxury, too. . . . And I don't know if I could afford you . . .

Fritz Perls, after a while, sums up the dream:

Let me say something more about the dream altogether. You see, the whole idea of repression is nonsense. If you look, everything is there. Now the most important thing to understand is the idea of projection. Every dream or every story contains all the material we need. The difficulty is to understand the idea of fragmentation. All the different parts are distributed all over the place. A person, for instance, who has lost his eyes— who has a hole instead of eyes, will always find

82

the eyes in the environment. He will always feel the world is looking at him.

Now Nora's *projection* (emphasis added, H.M.R.) is the incomplete house. She doesn't experience herself in the beginning as an incomplete house. It is projected as if she is living in this house. But she herself is the incomplete house, she admits she has solid foundations and so on. If you're capable of projecting yourself totally into every little bit of the dream—and really *become* that thing—then you begin to reassimilate, to re-own what you have disowned, given away. The more you disown, the more impoverished you get. Here is an opportunity to take back. The projections often appears as something unpleasant—as a spider, or as a train, or as a dead house, an incomplete house. But if you realize, "This is my dream. I'm responsible for the dream. I painted this picture. Every part is me," then things begin to function and to come together, instead of being incomplete and fragmented. And very often the projection is not even visible, but it's obvious. If I have a staircase without railings it's obvious that the railings are somewhere in the dream but they're missing. They're not there. So where railings should be, there's a hole. So we can find here a very brave, maybe stubborn person who can make it. Okeh."[5]

This type of dream interpretation, as done very effectively by Perls, is nevertheless extremely exhausting both to patient and therapist. Even if your thera-

[5] Perls, *Gestalt Therapy Verbatim* (Utah: Real People Press, 1969).

pist happens to be a Gestalt* therapist you should not expect that he will employ the Gestalt approach to dreams in every session with you. It should also be noted here that the Gestalt method of dream interpretation works very well in group situations and it was there apparently that Fritz Perls was highly successful. His approach is somewhat similar to the existential notion of dream interpretation. Both schools stress the here-and-now situation of the patient *vis-à-vis* the dream, and view the dream very much as an illustration of what is currently happening to the patient.

Two elements are then important in your talking to the analyst: free association and dreams. These still form the fundamental material of psychoanalytic therapy.

Remember that you should restrict your discussion of the analytic situation to your analytic session itself. As I stressed earlier, any discussion of your dreams or other material with friends or family, even wife or husband, will hamper your progress. Married patients find this aspect of analysis especially difficult, and are often tempted to discuss their therapy with their mates. Analysands are difficult to live with, they are under much more pressure and strain than usual, and their mates often become impatient and curious about what is going on in the analysis. Sometimes it

---

* In Gestalt therapy the therapist *insists* on staying with the feelings and emotions of the patient in the *here-and-now* situation. No long life history of the patient is taken. There is a strong emphasis on the *present*.

might be beneficial if your wife or husband were to enter therapy, preferably with another therapist, because of the transference situation. You should discuss this with your mate and your therapist.

Chapter 5

HOW DO I FEEL ABOUT
MY THERAPIST?

One of the most fundamental concepts of analysis is the phenomenon of transference. Simply stated, the patient *transfers* to the analyst certain feelings he once had for his parents or other major figures in his life. In the classical psychoanalytic situation the analyst functions as a *screen* against which the patient acts out these feelings.

According to Freud, patients want to express in action—reproduce in the real-life relationship with the analyst—infantile feelings for their parents that have been repressed. They want to "act them out," but they do not know what they are doing. Their acting out is an indication that they resist any consciousness of the feelings they had for their parents early in life. These repressed feelings now hide behind the feelings for the analyst. The psychoanalytic cure is designed to uncover this aim of acting out. The patient is encouraged to remember feelings he had for infantile love objects, but to remember *only*. He is to retain these feelings within the mental sphere, and eventually the transference must be overcome.[1]

---

[1] Sigmund Freud, "Observations on Transference-Love," *Standard Edition*, vol. XII.

This is accomplished by showing the patient that his feelings do not originate in the current situation, and do not really concern the person of the physician, but that he is reproducing something that had happened to him long ago. In this way, we require him to transform his *repetition* into recollection.[2]

The implication is that only by frustrating the acting out can the patient be brought to remember infantile love objects and thus detach himself gradually from the transference situation.

There is little doubt among analysts today that we have moved away from Freud's original concepts on the transference situation. How far we may have moved is uncertain, but some indication of just how far we have gone is given in Orr's paper, "Transference and Countertransference: A Historical Survey," where he sums it up this way: "Most, if not all, recent psychoanalytic articles concerned with technique agree that handling of the transference continues to be the *sine qua non* of the treatment."[3] But things were changing. "Increasingly," Orr says, ". . . 'handling' is taken to mean 'manipulation' in one form or another, and with the intensity of the transference or the depth of the therapeutic regression the points at issue." And although Orr could say that "the development, interpretation and resolution of the trans-

[2] Sigmund Freud, *A General Introduction to Psychoanalysis* (New York: Doubleday & Company, 1943), p. 461.

[3] D. Orr. "Transference and Countertransference: A Historical Survey," *Journal of the American Psychoanalytic Association*, 1954, 2:621–670.

ference neurosis in the analytic relationship is still the hallmark of psychoanalysis for perhaps a majority of analysts today," he added the qualification that "for a considerable minority this is by no means the case, or at least not without considerable attenuation and modification."[4]

By 1976 therefore, it seems possible that a great many analysts may have already abandoned rigid conceptions of the transference neurosis. The extent of this evolution should not be surprising. Freud himself seems to have anticipated even from the beginning that such a process would occur, for in a 1905 paper, he states, "This [the transference] happens . . . to be by far the hardest part of the whole task."[5] Then he adds this most remarkable sentence: "It is easy to learn how to interpret dreams, to extract from the patient's associations his unconscious thought and memories and to practice similar explanatory arts. . . ." This short statement was intended to be a warning. The transference, Freud implies, is so hard to work with that we will be tempted to attenuate, modify, or even omit it. But if we do this, the warning goes on, analysis will be reduced to explanatory art. The general sense of this warning seems clear, but Freud's stated reason for the great difficulty of working with transference scarcely matches the seriousness of the warning. "Transference," he says, ". . . has to be detected almost without assistance and with only the slightest clues. . . ."

[4] Orr, "Transference and Countertransference," p. 646.

[5] Sigmund Freud, "Fragment of an Analysis of a Case of Hysteria," *Standard Edition,* vol. VII, p. 116.

Is that all there is to it? Or was Freud's warning prompted by another reason? Is he neatly writing about how very hard it is *on the analyst* to work effectively with the transference neurosis? We forget sometimes that a neurosis is based upon conflict and that what is specific about a transference neurosis is the active involvement of the analyst in the crux of this conflict. This abrasive, emotionally draining experience is surely one of the major reasons some analysts back away from the transference neurosis and away from analysis itself. Yet if analysis is to proceed successfully, if a transference neurosis is to develop and be analyzed, the analyst cannot back off, cannot merely sit back, observe, interpret, and "practice similar explanatory arts." In addition, via the influence of the analytic situation, the patient must be enabled to include the analyst in his neurosis, or, as it were, to share his neurosis with the analyst. Only in this way, it seems, can the patient effectively reawaken the early stages of his neurosis; only in this way can its latent parts and forces be rendered sufficiently identifiable to be available for analysis.

Before moving on to other views on the transference situation, it might be helpful to quote a Freudian analyst, who, in an interview with Adelaide Bry, affirms some of the previous observations on transference:

Dr. Hammett—In analysis we take any feeling that the patient has about us as being not determined by our actual personality and who we actually are, but as being something that the patient felt earlier in life for some other important person, as for example, toward the father or the mother, or a brother or a sister, which he is transferring to us in the treatment context. Now if he sat up and faced us and talked to us that way, we would be very real individuals to him, and he would probably react to us to a considerable extent in terms of what we really are.

Adelaide Bry—Would that be helpful?

Dr. Hammett—Not in doing analysis, because in analysis we are trying to help the patient find out what happened earlier in his life, perhaps with his father or mother or both, that is still affecting him and making him sick. So that when we sit out of sight of him, we become a rather nonexistent, somewhat unreal person, and what then comes into his mind are fantasies and memories from the past which he displaces onto us, or transfers onto us without realizing that it comes from his past. A typical example of this would be a male patient who might have had an inordinate fear of his father and his father's discipline and anger. He might well develop an unrealistic fear of the analyst with the idea that the analyst was very disapproving, harsh, and so on.

Adelaide Bry—You mean because you're so quiet and out of sight, he must be making all this up in his mind?

Dr. Hammett—That's right. It's coming up in

his mind from the past and he is transferring it to us because we are the only other person there.[6]

Now contrast this with the attitude of the existential analyst toward transference. The existential analyst does not believe that the theoretical assumptions leading to Freud's suggestions are correct. According to the existential analyst, Freud does not prove convincingly that the patient's feelings for the analyst do not arise from the *present* situation, does not prove that they are directed, not toward the analyst, but "really" toward the patient's father or mother. Freud, the existentialists claim, even proves the contrary. First, he admits that "one has no right to dispute the genuine nature of the love which makes its appearance in the course of analytic treatment." Secondly, he confesses, in a different context, that a correct interpretation of an emotional attachment to the analyst as "transference" from somewhere else, or of acting out as "transference-resistance," does not produce the results we expect from correct interpretations of neurotic behavior—namely, the cessation of it. Freud says:

. . . giving the resistance a name could not result in its immediate cessation. One must allow the patient time to become more conversant with this resistance with which he has now become acquainted, *to work through* it, to overcome it, by continuing, in defiance of it. . . . The doctor

---
[6] Adelaide Bry (ed.), *Inside Psychotherapy* (New York: Basic Books, 1972), pp. 14–15.

has nothing else to do *than to wait and let things take their course* (emphasis added, H.M.R.), a course which cannot be avoided nor always hastened.[7]

In contrast to Freud, the existential analyst knows beforehand that the so-called transference does not "transfer" anything. He also knows that cures are not effected by months of "working through," during which the supposed meaning of the patient's relationship to the analyst and of his acting out are drilled into him. The existential analyst considers transference love or hate as the *genuine* feelings and emotions the analysand experiences toward the analyst. The fact that the patient behaves in an infantile manner, and therefore misjudges the actual situation to a large extent (because of his emotional immaturity, which in turn is rooted in his youth), does not detract from the *genuineness* of his present feelings. The patient begins to love the analyst as soon as he becomes aware that he has found someone—possibly for the first time in his life—who really understands him and who accepts him even though he is stunted by his neurosis. He loves him all the more because the analyst permits him to unfold more fully his real, essential being within a safe, interpersonal relationship on the "playground of transference." Existential analysts believe that all genuine love of one person for another is based on the possibility that the loved one offers to the lover

[7] Sigmund Freud, "Remembering, Repeating and Working-Through," *Standard Edition*. vol. XII, p. 155.

for a fuller unfolding of his own being by being in the world with him.

On the other hand, the patient will hate his analyst if he is still (because of his childhood experiences) limited to a child-father or child-mother relationship which restricts his perception of adults. He will hate him even more—and with good reason—if the analyst, because of a neurotically restricted emotional attitude (countertransference) toward the patient, actually behaves like one of the formerly hated parents.

Existential analysts, it is important for you to know, differ fundamentally from the Freudians on the concepts of transference and acting out. Freud has undoubtedly given us a masterful description of the way resistances against the acquisition of hitherto feared possibilities of living melt in what he called the "fire of transference-love." But—and here is the existential analyst talking—when the patient wants not only to think or talk about his relation to the analyst but also wants to experience his *newly discovered* possibilities in the language of his emotions and his body, Freud called this the "acting-out of resistance." The existential analyst differs from Freud on this point. To the existential analyst, the desire for emotional and physical acting out appears as much a part of the newly sprouting possibilities for relating as do the thoughts that belong to these possibilities. Therefore, the exisential analyst cannot regard such acting out as a repetition—in action—of repressed infantile emotions of love or hate toward a parent, or even as resistance against becoming conscious of such old "love objects." He will therefore carefully avoid transforming the so-called acting out into "psychic material," namely into remembering and verbal expression. On the contrary, he will let the acting out continue to the greatest extent possible without violating his own integrity, inner freedom, and concern for his patient. He will, as an existential analyst, do this because he regards acting out as a *genuine* phenomenon—as, more often than not, the very opposite of an attempt to repress. Acting out may indicate that something is unfolding for the *very first time* in the life of the patient. He dares to behave in a manner that had never before been permitted him. Acting out in these cases can neither be a remembering or a repetition. The existential analyst will therefore allow his patient to act out in this manner, feeling that it is therapeutically effective for the patient to do so.

It is interesting to note here that Freud contradicted his own definition of transference (as an "erroneous linkage of an affect and an object") when he stated that "one has no right to dispute the genuine nature of love which makes its appearance in the course of analytic treatment." Freud the therapist, moreover, behaved in actual treatment as if he were cognizant of these existential insights. He admonished the analyst to "wait and let things take their course," because in all patients capable of sublimation, the process of healing usually "takes place from within as soon as their inhibitions have been removed by the analysis." These phrases imply that the concept of "working through" is primarily a theoretical screen for permissiveness in regard to the trying out and practicing of newly accepted ways of behaving in the analyst-patient relationship.

Having discussed these essential concepts of transference as conceived by Freudian and existential therapies, we turn to the question of how you *yourself* can recognize what is happening when transference sets in. Remember that transference is expressed in positive and negative fashions. By arriving late or wanting to cancel your session, you might express resistance, which in turn is connected with your feelings for your therapist. Or you might want to stay longer at one of your sessions, "being the good patient" to please your therapist, bring him small presents, question him about himself and his family, try to telephone him, pay him in advance, dress up for him, find out the date of his birthday so that you can send him a card—in short, get his attention. All of this amounts to transference, which will have to be discussed in one form or another, depending on your therapist's orientation.

In the meantime it is well for you to be aware that the therapist also experiences feelings for you. Those feelings can be positive or negative, but he must deal with those feelings himself. He has *no right* to impose those feelings on you in the analytic situation. Some analysts believe that sharing these feelings might be important for the therapeutic situation, but this is a very delicate matter. How is the therapist to know that his feelings are not going to affect the patient's therapeutic situation? Has he sorted out his own feelings? Only a psychoanalyst who has been very well analyzed himself would be capable of handling such a situation. Unfortunately there is an increasing number of analysts today who express their own negative and positive feelings to their patients, often to the surprise of the patient, who usually has no idea how to handle a situation of this sort.

Freud warned against this:

> He (the analyst) has evoked this love (transference-love) by instituting analytic treatment in order to cure the neurosis. For him, it is an unavoidable consequence of a medical situation, like the exposure of a patient's body or the imparting of a vital secret. It is therefore plain to him that he must not derive *any personal advantage* (emphasis added, H.M.R.) from it. The patient's willingness makes no difference; it merely throws the whole responsibility on the analyst himself.[8]

Patients who fall in love with their analysts should realize what Freud said:

> For the doctor, *ethical motives* (emphasis added, H.M.R.) unite with the technical ones to restrain him from giving the patient his love. The aim he has to keep in view is that this woman, whose capacity for love is impaired by infantile fixations, should gain free command over a function which is of such inestimable importance to her; that she should not, however, dissipate it in the treatment, but keep it ready for the time when,

8 Sigmund Freud, "Observations on Transference-Love," *Standard Edition*, vol. XII, p. 169.

after her treatment, the demands of real life make themselves felt.[9]

The statement could not be clearer. Analysts have to prepare their patients for the world. Any other situation—where the analyst and the patient engage in activities not pertinent to the *therapeutic* situation —is a rationalization on the part of the therapist in order to take advantage of the patient.

You should also recognize your analyst cannot prepare you for either transference or countertransference; even if the analyst is very skilled you will pick up some of his countertransference. As Freud stated:

It has come to my knowledge that some doctors who practice analysis frequently prepare their patients for the emergence of the erotic transference or even urge them to "go ahead and fall in love with the doctor so that the treatment may make progress." I can hardly imagine a more senseless proceeding. In doing so, analyst robs the phenomenon of the element of spontaneity which is so convincing and lays up obstacles for himself in the future which are hard to overcome.[10]

And further on, Freud calls it

just as disastrous for the analysis if the patient's craving for love is gratified as if it is suppressed.

---

[9] Freud, "Observations on Transference-Love," p. 169.
[10] Freud, "Observations on Transference-Love," p. 161.

The course the analyst must pursue is neither of these; it is one for which there is no model in real life. He must take care not to steer away from the transference-love, or to repulse it or to make it distasteful to the patient; but he must just as resolutely withhold any response to it. He must keep firm hold of the transference-love, but treat it as something unreal, as a situation which has to be gone through in the treatment and traced back to its unconscious origins and which must assist in bringing all that is most deeply hidden in the patient's erotic life into her consciousness and therefore under *her control* (emphasis added, H.M.R.).[11]

As a patient you should realize—as should the analyst—that every transference situation provokes a countertransference situation, which arises from the analyst's identification of himself with the patient's (internal) objects, a phenomenon called complementary countertransference. These countertransference situations may be repressed or emotionally blocked, but probably cannot be avoided; certainly they should not be avoided if full understanding is to be achieved.

We also know that every positive transference situation is answered by a positive countertransference; to every negative transference there responds, in one part of the analyst, a negative countertransference. It is of great importance that the analyst be conscious of this law, for awareness of it is fundamental to

[11] Freud, "Observations on Transference-Love," p. 166.

avoid "drowning" in the countertransference. If he is not aware of it he will not be able to avoid entering into the vicious circle of the patient's neurosis, a situation that will hinder or even prevent the work of analysis.

For example, if the patient's neurosis centers on a conflict with his introjected father, he will project the father upon the analyst and treat the latter as his father; the analyst will feel treated as such—he will feel treated badly—and he will react internally, in a part of his personality, in accordance with the treatment he receives. If the analyst fails to be aware of this reaction, his behavior will inevitably be affected by it, and the situations that, to a greater or lesser degree, helped to establish the patient's neurosis will be repeated. Hence it is of the greatest importance that the analyst develop within himself what might be termed an *ego observer* of his countertransference reactions, which are, naturally, continuous. Perception of these countertransference reactions will help him to become conscious of the continuous transference situations of the patient and to interpret them rather than be unconsciously ruled by these reactions, as not infrequently happens. A well-known example is the "revengeful silence" of the analyst. If the analyst is unaware of these reactions there is danger that the patient will have to repeat, in his transference experience, the vicious circle brought about by the introjection and projection of "bad objects" (in reality neurotic ones) and the consequent pathological anxieties and defenses; but transference interpretations made possible by the analyst's awareness of his countertransference also make it possible to open important breaches in this vicious circle.

If you do feel that you are falling in love with your analyst, remember that your insistence on his returning your love is part of the analytic situation, no matter what kind of analysis you are in.

In writing on the transference situation Freud made clear that:

> . . . it (transference-love) is provoked by the *analytic situation* (emphasis added, H.M.R.); secondly, it is greatly intensified by the resistance, which dominates the situation; and thirdly, it is lacking to a high degree in a regard for reality, is less sensible, less concerned about consequences and more blind in its valuation of the loved person that we are prepared to admit in the case of normal love.[12]

So your love for him is part of the analytic situation. You most probably would never have fallen in love with him if it were not that you had entered analysis with him.

It is important that you get yourself an analyst who is aware and in control of his own countertransference; otherwise he may do you great harm. Only well-analyzed therapists, those who are very much in touch with themselves, who have successfully

---

[12] Freud, "Observations on Transference-Love, pp. 168–69.

worked through their personal problems, and are happy sexually and emotionally are likely to be able to give you what you need in the analytic treatment you have undertaken.

Chapter 6

HOW LONG IS THIS GOING TO LAST?:
DIAGNOSIS AND PROGNOSIS

It has become popular among contemporary psychoanalytic patients to speculate upon their diagnosis.
This is partly due to the superficial knowledge many
patients have today of psychoanalysis and psychology.
However, is the knowledge of your diagnosis going
to benefit your treatment? No, it will not, because,
as is well known among psychotherapists, such knowledge is used by the patient as a defense against further
progress. In not telling you the diagnosis, your therapist is not playing hide-and-seek with you, but is acting
solely in your own interests. Moreover, those patients who already have a sound knowledge of psychoanalysis because of their own professional background,
psychologists and social workers, for example, discover that their knowledge is often a handicap in
the therapeutic situation. They tend to intellectualize
far more than the patient who comes to the therapeutic situation *unprepared* for what he is going to
experience or discover.

Obviously your condition is going to determine the
length of the therapy. Here again, the therapist will
not always be able to share with you his opinion
about the length of your analysis. A great deal de-

pends on your willingness to work hard, how well motivated you are, and the degree of your commitment to the therapy. Sloppy work on your part, such as missed appointments, continuous resistance, and a generally lazy attitude will delay the termination of your treatment.

Freud covered the question of the length of the treatment as follows:

An unwelcome question which the patient asks the doctor at the outset is: "How long will the treatment take? How much time will you need to relieve me of my trouble?" If one has proposed a trial treatment of a few weeks one can avoid giving a direct answer to this question by promising to make a more reliable pronouncement at the end of the trial period. Our answer is like the answer given by the Philosopher to the Wayfarer in Aesop's fable. When the Wayfarer asked how long a journey lay ahead, the Philosopher merely answered "Walk!" and afterwards explained his apparently unhelpful reply on the ground that he must know the length of the Wayfarer's stride before he could tell how long his journey would take. This expedient helps one over the first difficulties; but the comparison is not a good one, for the neurotic can easily alter his pace and may at times make only very slow progress. In point of fact, the question as to the probable duration of a treatment is almost unanswerable.[1]

[1] Sigmund Freud, "On Beginning the Treatment," *Standard Edition*, Vol. XII, p. 128.

If you are in an ongoing depth analysis you will discover that progress occurs at the most unexpected moments. Don't forget that you absorb the analytic treatment and that the rewards often come at moments when you least expect them. You suddenly discover that you can handle a certain situation much better than in the past, that you are more decisive and more assertive, more aggressive, if you will, and that you feel good about these changes in yourself.

In short-term, supportive therapy, results often manifest themselves sooner than in in-depth analysis because of the attitude of the therapist, who often is directive and assertive. The question of how long these results will last remains to a large extent unanswerable.

There will be times during your therapy when you feel like quitting or perhaps taking a break. This is usually interpreted as resistance on the part of the patient and hence must be explored in the therapeutic situation. Breaks in the therapy are bad inasmuch as the *consistency* of the analysis becomes interrupted, which can only be to your disadvantage.

Freud writes this about the interruption of the analysis:

I do not bind patients to continue the treatment for a certain length of time; I allow each one to break off whenever he likes. But *I do not hide* (emphasis added, H.M.R.) it from him that if the treatment is stopped after only a small amount of work has been done it will not be successful and may easily, like an unfinished operation, leave him in an unsatisfactory state.[2]

In an almost capricious afterthought Freud writes, "In the early years of my psycho-analytic practice I used to have the greatest difficulty in prevailing on my patients to continue their analysis. This difficulty has long since been shifted, and I now have to take the greatest pains to induce them to give it up."

You will find over and over again that you want to speed up the therapy. Even in the early years of psychoanalysis various pupils of Freud devised ways to shorten the analysis. Ferenczi suggested that the analyst set a date for termination, but later changed his mind. Freud himself, in the case of the Wolf Man, experimented with setting dates for termination, but finally decided against doing so.

Ferenczi felt that he could possibly shorten certain analyses by the introduction of his "active therapy," what he termed the "systematic issuing and carrying out of *commands* and of *prohibitions*."[3] He also felt that in some cases the analyst should "encourage or discourage patients directly towards or against production of *thoughts* and phantasies."[4] This active intervention, incidentally, which is intended to shorten the analysis, is quite similar to what some of the encounter

---

[2] Freud, "On Beginning the Treatment," p. 129.

[3] Sándor Ferenczi, "The Further Development of an Active Therapy in Psychoanalysis" in *Further Contributions to the Theory and Technique of Psychoanalysis* by Sándor Ferenczi (New York: Basic Books, 1960), p. 206.

[4] Ferenczi, "The Further Development of an Active Therapy in Psychoanalysis," p. 207.

and Gestalt therapist have suggested during the last decade.

Any break in analysis or even in short-term supportive therapy should be discussed by you and your therapist. Interruptions in the therapeutic process often are detrimental to your chances for a successful outcome. Frequent interruptions, even missing a few appointments, tend to break up that process of growth and will slow down the pace of your therapy.

You should, if at all possible, schedule your vacation for the time when your therapist is also on vacation. He will tell you far in advance when he is going to take off and will prepare you for it. On the whole it is not advisable for either the patient or the therapist to take a great number of short vacations. It is much better and more productive for both therapist and patient to take one long vacation during the summer and perhaps another short one in the winter.

Inasmuch as you, as a patient, should not cancel your appointments or take off at the drop of a hat, the therapist should abide by the same rule. He is also thus restricted in his social life in that he cannot just go off on a holiday whenever he feels like it. He should keep the cancellation of appointments on his part to an absolute minimum. Analytic patients become greatly upset when the routine and consistency of the analysis are broken. You will discover, after you have been in therapy a while, that any upset in the schedule of your therapist will prove to be very disturbing to you. A sudden departure of your therapist, even for a short time, will throw you, as will any extended illness or especially the death of your therapist.

Also bear in mind that except for emergencies your absent or unavailable therapist cannot really be replaced by one of his colleagues. The reason? Because he knows more about you and your case than any colleague could, and about all that his replacement can do is to hold your hand.

Therapists have a firm commitment to their patients, and most of them recognize this and will keep interruptions of the therapy on their part to an absolute minimum. If for one reason or another your therapist must terminate his practice, he then has a moral obligation to prepare you thoroughly for that move and to suggest another therapist to you. Such occurrences are very unfortunate. The patient, who must begin again with someone else, will justifiably feel bitterly resentful about his therapist's departure. In some, though not all, cases, he will literally have to start all over again. Because of the very private and transferential aspects of the analytic situation, the patient will have to establish once again from the very beginning a unique relationship, which has just been taken away from him.

Interestingly enough, some of the early analysts, Freud among them, were so committed to their patients that they would often take one or two of analysands on vacation with them. Freud always insisted, however, that the patient stay not in the village where he was spending his vacation, but in another community nearby. Today this practice has disappeared.

An important reason for your desire to leave therapy might be the improvement in your life situation as a result of the therapy. Ferenczi warns against the "half-cured" patient:

> Freud has already pointed out that therapeutic success is often a hindrance to the thoroughness of the analysis; I was able to substantiate this in a number of cases. It may easily happen, if the irksome symptoms of the neurosis disappear during analytic treatment, that the still manifest indications of illness seem less troublesome to the patient than the continuation of the work of the analysis, which is often so hard and so full of renunciations. Should, however, the treatment really become *peior morbo,* the patient hastens (mostly also compelled by material considerations) to break it off and directs his interest to real life which he already finds satisfying. Such half-cured people in any case are usually still attached to their doctor by the bonds of transference; one learns that they talk somewhat exaggeratedly about the treatment and the person of the doctor, and they give indications, too, from time to time of their continued existence by picture postcards or other little attentions, in contradistinction to those patients who broke off the treatment in the minds of the resistance and wrap themselves in obstinate silence. The really cured, whose transference was dissolved, have no need to bother themselves particularly about their doctor, and do not do so.[5]

---

[5] Sándor Ferenczi, "Discontinuous Analyses," in *Further Contributions,* p. 233.

The termination of analysis has proved to be one of the most crucial elements in the analytic situation. There is a popular, but distorted notion, that analysts keep their patients around (for financial reasons) and that they really do not want to terminate them. I have always considered that notion a rather ridiculous one. As one who has been in practice for quite a number of years, I really cannot see how an analyst *wants* to keep patients around forever. For those analysts who see their patients for a five-year time span it is a relief to move on to someone else. What has happened is that the uninformed public usually views long analyses as unsuccessful ones. That point should be disputed also. Depending on the severity of the patient's neurosis and on how well he is working through his problems, his termination time will be determined by the degree of improvement and his ability to handle himself successfully in the world.

Long analyses are sometimes necessary; oten they are what we call *maintenance* therapies, and one should only commend the stamina and patience of the analyst who can put up with this kind of analysis. Some patients will simply never leave therapy, and will need the analytic process in order to function reasonably well in the society in which they live. I see nothing wrong with that. It seems to me that it is better than nonfunctioning, or worse, the mental hospital. The argument of dependency, so often heard in pseudo-analytic circles, is also ridiculous. We are dependent on many things in our society, and we can never achieve total independency, even if it were desirable. People are also dependent on a family structure that in many ways resembles their childhood dependency on mother or father or both. Are we therefore rejecting the institution of marriage or, for that matter, other alternative life-styles where a certain dependency plays a role?

There are various methods for the termination of the analysis. Obviously the patient should be prepared for the termination, and it is up to the analyst to do so. However, there are many opinions as to how to go about this. As mentioned earlier, Freud at one time believed that a termination should be set at the outset, but later changed his mind. Laforgue, a well-known French analyst and an analysand of Freud, would set a tentative date. Ferenczi finally believed, after considering and working with a firm termination date, that the analysis must "die of exhaustion." Franz Alexander proposed one or more preparatory interruptions of one to eighteen months. Buxbaum strongly favored an "open-door" policy, whereby the patient is encouraged to return for a visit. Karl Menninger accepts the patient's ruminations about termination and lets it be known that he does not feel these are resistances. If he sensed no "protest symptoms" he would speak in more definite terms of an exact time of termination.

In the actual process of preparing the patient for termination the analyst should encourage the patient to drop one or two of his sessions and so gradually taper off the analysis. The patient should be told that he has earned the termination, that work on certain problems still needs to be done, but that the analyst is now relying on the patient to do this himself.

The criteria for ending an analysis were carefully considered by Freud in his celebrated paper, "Analysis Terminable and Interminable." According to Freud:

We must first of all decide what is meant by the ambiguous phrase "the end of an analysis." From a practical standpoint it is easy to answer. An analysis is ended when the analyst and the patient cease to meet each other for the analytic session. This happens when two conditions have been approximately fulfilled: first, that the patient shall no longer be suffering from his symptoms and shall have overcome his anxieties and his inhibitions; and secondly, that the analyst shall judge that so much repressed material has been made conscious, so much that was unintelligible has been explained, and so much internal resistance conquered, that there is no need to fear a repetition of the pathological processes concerned. If one is prevented by external difficulties from reaching this goal, it is better to speak of an *incomplete* analysis rather than of an *unfinished* one.[6]

Again, one can extend Freud and consider the following criteria when termination is considered. There should be enough evidence of the patient's ability to control, retard, or reduce the frequency and intensity of his symptoms. In other words, the patient should have reached the point where he can determine and

[6] Sigmund Freud, "Analysis Terminable and Interminable," *Standard Edition*, vol. XXIII, p. 219.

have an impact upon the intensity of the symptoms. There should be less inhibition in his speech, association of ideas, motor movements, and a considerable abatement of self-destructive behavior. There should actually be "surprises" in the strength of his interpersonal relationships. There should also be a lessening of maladaptive behavior patterns he might have demonstrated in the analysis. For example, if there has been a pattern, of coming late to appointments, he should begin to arrive on time; or if he has been a "hanger-on," he should give up his habit of asking, "One more question before I leave."

By now he should have developed a good tolerance of the necessary interruptions of the analysis, such as vacation breaks. He should start to reveal impressions, misunderstandings, distortions, or secrets about the analyst dating back to the initial interview. There should be spontaneity in associations, with little amnesia, and a good measure of satisfaction in work performance.

He should also have developed a reasonable tolerance of the problems of others. Conversely, he should be sufficiently assertive to set limits on the behavior of others that should not be tolerated. He should be resourceful in the use of his free time with a minimum of daily rituals and a genuine feeling of choice about those that remain. He should have developed a natural consistency in his sexual performance or an acceptance of his capacities in this area. His dreams now become shorter and he is able to recall them with greater facility and completeness. He shows an ability to laugh at himself in a way that invites others to join in.

At this time, too, he makes repeated inquiries about termination of the analysis. Neither the first nor the second need be heeded, but the third possibly should be respected. That the question of termination is very much on his mind might be confirmed by dreams or allusions to individual developmental experiences involving the loss of a key person.

There are, of course, clues the analyst himself may experience about the approaching termination. He might feel, for example, a sense of pleasant contemplation about an approaching hour with the patient. He might experience feelings of satisfaction concerning the basic capacity for responsive human relations and respect for the emotional strength of the patient. He will see a sharp contrast between the patient's problems when treatment was begun and his current problems.

He should also have confidence that the patient can handle future stressful situations. There is a possibility that the analyst might experience a *paradoxical* reaction of boredom, depression, or feelings of competitiveness with the patient. He might also feel that he has learned something.

Finally, he should be aware of a category of phenomena one might label "Beware of Thin Ice." Termination should not be considered if, after a period of long and intensive analysis, the patient begins to express complaints about the fee and chronic disagreements with the hour of the appointment, or provocatively misses or cancels appointments. Precipitous shifts to a superficial discussion of problems or a denial of all problems are also signs that indicate termination should not be considered. These particular signs are often reflected in a reporting of the chronology of happenings between analytic sessions, desire to leave the therapist before being "abandoned," the expression of wishes to meet the analyst socially "when the analysis is over," or the reverse: "I never want to see you again when the analysis is over."

Once the patient is confronted with the termination, he will react in the analytic sessions. One of the most remarkable developments possible at this stage is that the patient will try to repeat (or sometimes actually does repeat) the problems he demonstrated early in the analysis. There is a recrudescence, or a *da capo*. The patient plays through the chorus again. If the analyst has correctly assessed the potential for the closing phase of the therapeutic relationship, there should be little wavering on his part. Some inexperienced analysts, however, might relinquish their program for termination under the onslaught of a patient's dependency transference. In a sense the patient will experience the termination as the loss of a key person in his life. Mourning and separation anxiety will be experienced as part of the termination stage.

Another significant pretermination reaction that requires discussion is the paradoxically deep insight that may occur in the patient at this phase of the analysis. Such an occurrence supports the idea that the termination phase may contribute as much to the result of the analysis as the initial stage does. At the time that

Freud felt that fixing a date for termination of analysis put the necessary pressure on the patient, he cited an example (the Wolf Man) that led him to this conclusion: "It was a case of the patient himself obstructing the cure: the analysis was in danger of failing as a result of its—partial—success." The patient in question "had made progress in independency, his relations to principal people in his life were adjusted, and interest in life was awakened. However, there was no progress in clearing up his childhood neurosis, the basis of his later illness."

Similar plateaus in the progress of analysis are frequently observed. Motivation toward resolution of problems may come only in the termination process. Freud indicated to the patient in question that "the coming year was to be the last of his analysis." The patient was then able to "produce all the memories and to discover the connecting links which were necessary for the understanding of his early neurosis."

Rank, who favored short analyses, also approved of setting the termination date early in the analysis so that the knowledge of the end would not be received as a shock. On the other hand, he also expressed himself in favor of letting the patient or circumstances set the time of termination. And he said, "The analyst may push a little to help but should let the actual arrival of the end be a natural outgrowth. In using this technique it is surprising to find that the patient usually reaches the end more quickly than he would if the analyst had set the time."

Today, most therapists will favor a mutual agreement on the termination date. What is important is that you start to discuss your termination early enough with your therapist so that you can prepare yourself for the end of the analysis. Even after you are finished with the analysis, you will experience something of a separation anxiety and you may still wonder "how he is doing?" Gradually, however, you will see, provided your analysis has been successful, that you feel that you are really on your own and have no need of talking about your problems.

In the end you will assess the results of your treatment and you will probably experience far more growth and actual results after your analysis is over than during it, because now you have the tools, the insight, knowledge, and strength, to do it all yourself.

Chapter 7

SHOULD I GET INTO A GROUP?

The last decade has witnessed a tremendous upsurge of interest in group psychotherapy in the United States. Often patients who are in individual psychotherapy do not feel the need to participate in group psychotherapy. They feel that their experience in individual psychotherapy is sufficient. Many other patients, however, think differently, and are eager to make group therapy a part of their therapeutic experience.

When you are already in individual therapy and you are interested in entering a group, the logical step is to ask your own analyst about it. Perhaps he conducts groups himself, although a substantial number of psychoanalysts do not conduct group therapy nor have they been trained to do so. Most orthodox therapists, as you will find out, stay away from the experience of group therapy. It has never been considered a major therapeutic tool by orthodox therapists, and group therapy is not included in the required training of their psychoanalytic institutes. Most of them do not even consider group therapy an adjunct of individual therapy. If you find yourself in treatment with such an analyst and in the course of your analysis you express the desire to enter some form of group therapy, it is unlikely that he will have serious objections. But then again, he might well insist that you concentrate on the individual therapeutic experience in which you are involved. If he consents to your entering a group he will most likely warn you against becoming involved with an untrained group therapist.

How do you find out if your group therapist is qualified? In recent years the group therapist has emerged as a separate professional *identity*. The increasing demand for group therapy and the inability of many individual therapists to handle this demand have resulted in the appearance of therapists who tend to specialize solely in group therapy. The group therapist who is well trained has been part of the group therapy experience himself and has conducted groups, when in training, under qualified supervision. He should also be a member of the American Group Psychotherapy Association, which sets high standards in terms of training and supervision for its members. If your prospective group therapist is not a member of the AGPA you may consider staying away, since the field of group therapy is rampant with amateurs. Yet, there are undoubtedly many group therapists who have had sufficient training, but for one reason or another are not members of the AGPA. You will have to decide for yourself whether you want to go ahead with such a group therapist.

If you are in individual analysis and your therapist happens to conduct groups himself, he probably will insist, if you have expressed the desire to enter a group, that you participate in one of his groups and not go to one conducted by someone else. Most therapists in that kind of situation prefer to have their patients in both individual and group analysis with them. The analyst thus gains a unique insight into your functioning as a group member and thus, possibly, into your problems in general. For you, in turn, it might be a valuable experience, in terms of your relationship with your therapist, to see him active in a group experience. Because of the nature of the group experience, he will show other and perhaps surprising sides of himself in the group. If your therapist does not have room for you in any of his groups he might then refer you to one of his colleagues; such referrals are quite common.

Before discussing the nature of the group experience and the question of qualifying for the group experience, a practical matter should be discussed briefly. Fees for group therapy vary, but you will probably be charged between $15 and $30 per one-and-a-half-hour session, depending upon the experience and reputation of the group therapist. Most groups meet once a week, although some might meet twice a week, or they might even meet once a week without the therapist as a kind of supplementary session. Of course there are many variations. Some groups might meet for two or three hours; others have no particular time limit.

The most important question for you is, "Do I qualify for group?" and for that matter you might ask yourself why your therapist has not invited you to join one of his groups. In order to qualify for group, most therapists agree, you should have had some individual therapy and your therapist must be sure that you can withstand the pressures that are sometimes brought against you in the therapeutic group experience. In other words, patients with fragile egos are not likely to be good group candidates. Neither are psychotics and psychopaths. As in individual psychotherapy, neurotics are the best candidates for group therapy since they are able to produce and relate, although with limitations.

Your therapist might also feel that the burden of individual therapy is quite enough for you, or at a given point in time he might consider that individual therapeutic experience more crucial for your growth than the group experience. However, with the increasing interest in group therapy and the emergence of the encounter group therapies, patients are now more apt to pressure their therapists to initiate group experiences for them.

If you are in analysis with a more traditional or even an existential analyst, your group experience with him will be in the tradition of individual psychoanalysis. Conventional group psychotherapy holds that the same process that takes place in individual therapy occurs, although in another form, in the group experience. In other words, such phenomena as transference, resistance, free association, and dream analysis are as much a part of the group therapeutic experience. In such a setting you will see that the group therapist is quite passive. Although he might intervene at times, as in individual analysis it is up to the patients to produce the material, and the tool of free association, so essential to individual analysis, is very much employed in the more conventional groups.

So what is the advantage of such a group for you? You should realize that group therapy reflects in a larger sense the family structure and that you will start reacting in the group *as if* it were your family. The underlying dynamics that you encountered in your own family will be experienced all over again in the group. Thus the process of repetition so crucial to individual analysis also takes place here. Observing you as a part of that family can give your therapist additional hints as how to proceed with you in the individual analysis. He also might take the opportunity to confront you in the group with certain insights he has not yet presented to you in the individual session. Moreover, once in the group, you will discover that others have similar problems, which might be a comfort to you at times. You will interact with the other members of the group and you will consider them almost as members of your family. You might become very close to some members of the group, which raises some important questions.

Should you socialize with the members of your group? Should you sleep with them, if you want to? Some of these questions are somewhat the same as those raised in your individual therapy. Again the more conventional group therapist will recommend very strongly that the members of the group not socialize with each other. He will tell you that the same principle that governs individual therapy—that one should not dilute the material outside the therapeutic session

—is applicable to the group therapy session. He will state that conversations and involvements outside the group will take your activity and productivity away from the group. It is in the group itself that the action should take place, and the therapist may interpret your socializing with other members of the group as a form of resistance. The same, he feels, will apply to sexual involvements with members of the group. Since the group reflects the family, your sexual involvement with a member of the group might be characterized as incestuous and in the conventional group this would be considered a form of acting out.

Many group therapists no longer adhere to these strictures. They do not discourage socializing among members of the group, and although they will discuss the aspects of your eventual sexual involvements with members of the group, they certainly would not forbid you to become involved.

You might find yourself with a group therapist who is quite unconventional and who actually will participate in the group process himself. In other words, your group therapist becomes a regular member of the group. A prerequisite for such participation by the group therapist is that he should be well analyzed in order to avoid any serious projection on his part.

Conventional group therapy is usually an ongoing process and you will be in group as long as your own individual analysis lasts. As regards membership, there are two kinds of groups. The open group is a continuous group that will admit new members in the course of its existence. Members of the group will leave and others will appear. There are also closed groups, in which the members start together and preferably finish at the same time.

Groups usually have a membership of five to ten patients; the size will depend primarily on the practice of your therapist. If he has a large patient population he will usually have large groups and vice versa. Again, most of the principles that govern individual analysis apply to group psychoanalysis. Confidentiality, although much more difficult to handle because of the number of patients involved, should be strictly enforced. In other words, members of the group should not be talking to their friends about other members of the group.

As a result of the increasing popularity of group therapy in this country, we have seen a variety of groups and techniques emerge in recent years. There are groups that will meet for only a *limited* time, say a year. Others may be theme-oriented toward such specific topics as alienation, the search for identity, problems of creativity, sexual dysfunctioning, etc. There are groups for married couples, singles, homosexuals, lesbians, businessmen, or any other category of humanity sharing a common bond. Theme- or category-oriented groups are probably more likely to include patients who are not in individual analysis and do not desire to be in individual analysis. They view the group analysis as sufficient to deal with their problems. Many of those groups that contain patients who are not in individual analysis have turned into problem-solving groups rather than analytic groups. The patient is primarily bent on getting a quick solution for his problems and not all that interested in a deeper search into his sub- or unconscious.

That brings us to the matter of what kind of group you might be interested in. If you are a patient in individual analysis you probably are better off in a conventional group, but if you are married and have problems with your husband or wife you might consider a couples group. If you are not in analysis, you obviously have a wide variety of groups to choose from, and I shall briefly discuss here some of the advantages and disadvantages of these groups.[1]

The emergence of Gestalt groups, bio-energetic groups, sensitivity groups, consciousness-raising groups, and marathons has opened many new possibilities for you as a patient. For some patients it might indeed be very beneficial and productive to enter any one of these groups. On the whole, they provide *short-term* therapy in the field of group psychotherapy. For many people who are not particularly equipped to undertake any kind of depth analysis (either individual or group) these groups offer a viable alternative.

They focus very much on your present situation and do not delve into your past, and indeed, many of the therapists who lead these groups are not equipped for the latter because their training very often does not consist of an individual analysis or any kind of analytic training.

You should realize that many such therapists are insufficiently trained to handle matters of diagnosis or, for that matter, prognosis, and that membership in

---

[1] I have discussed the new group therapies in greater detail in my book *The New Group Therapies* (New York: Avon Books, 1970).

such a group entails many hazards in terms of your participation and interaction with your fellow patients in the group. Nevertheless it has been established that many of these new groups have been effective in solving some immediate life crises of their participants, although we do not know how long these solutions will sustain themselves in the absence of more fundamental depth analysis.

If you decide to enter any of these new groups you should go into one led by a qualified group therapist. You can easily check out his credentials. You can ask him yourself, and, if he seems uptight about answering your questions, you already have a warning. You can also consult the membership lists of the American Psychological Association, the American Academy of Psychotherapists, and the American Group Psychotherapy Association.

Nowadays, many argue that such qualifications do not necessarily make these persons into good therapists, but these qualifications are a necessary safeguard.

And now that you have been introduced to some ideas of what psychotherapy is all about, good luck on your therapeutic voyage!

Chapter 8

WHY DO THERAPISTS
CHARGE SO MUCH?

This is essentially a chapter about your analyst. What kind of man is he? Does he like his job? Why did he become an analyst? Is he rich? How can he endure a job like this?

Curiously, little has been written about the personality of the therapist, and we know really very little about the average analyst. Freud once remarked that neurotics make the best analysts, which does not necessarily mean that all analysts are *still* neurotic or perhaps ever were neurotic.

After all, all analysts have had a personal analysis as part of their analytic training, and although the personal analysis as a qualification for being an analyst has been questioned recently,[1] there is little doubt that a personal analysis is essential in order to perform well as an analyst. Of course, Abraham and Rank, two early pupils of Freud, were never analyzed, and they turned out to be very good analysts. But

[1] See David L. Rubinfine, "The Role of Personal Psychotherapy in the Training of Psychotherapists" and Arthur L. Leader, "The Argument Against Required Personal Analysis in Training for Psychotherapy." Both essays in Robert R. Holt (ed.), *New Horizons for Psychotherapy* (New York: International Universities Press, 1971).

then, most of the early analysts had brief and rather inconclusive analyses.[2] Freud himself often conducted analyses for no longer than three months (his so-called summer analyses for eager, young American analysts are a case in point).

It is obvious, of course, that in order to function well and treat you accordingly your analyst should have some measure of personal stability. Probably no analyst is free from personal problems, but as long as those problems do not interfere with his treatment of your situation you have nothing to worry about. You will have to worry when he starts talking compulsively about himself rather than about you! There is a currently popular notion that the analyst's introduction of his own life into the analytic situation will help the patient. I don't buy this. Only insofar as the personal material he introduces into the therapeutic situation is relevant to your condition can he be justified in doing so. Irrelevant material introduced by analysts is rationalization for a badly analyzed therapist to talk to you about his own problems and to project his neuroses upon you. That is not what you are paying him for. Such an analyst should return to analysis and get himself straightened out. In this respect Freud recommended very strongly that analysts go back into analysis every five years in order to get a better, more updated perspective of themselves.

In order to perform well as an analyst, the thera-

---

[2] Many early analysts, including Freud, considered the brief analyses enough of a tool to measure the ability of the analysand eventually to conduct his own practice.

pist should, as noted earlier, be relatively conflict-free, should have comfortable social and sexual relations, and be fairly liberated from the pressures of everyday life. He should certainly be sufficiently in touch with himself so that he knows where he is at, and he should have little confusion about his ongoing life situation.

Analysts who are in full-time practice should see to it that they are not continuously bothered by the petty details of daily existence. Any energy devoted to them will mean that the analyst is not fully prepared to devote his whole self to the therapeutic situation. One of the reasons that analysts must charge what many mistakenly think are unreasonably high fees is that they need to delegate a great many small tasks to secretaries or assistants. Many analysts tend to forget this and waste their time on unimportant details that could very well be taken care of by others who in fact may be better qualified for handling them than the analyst himself.

Being comfortable with one's own sexual and social situation is important for the analyst because it prevents him from projecting upon the therapeutic situation of his patient. One wonders if the current discussion of whether it is advisable for the analyst to sleep with his patient has more to do with the increased willingness of analysts to project their own unhappy domestic situations (and perhaps also bad personal analyses) upon their patients than it does with any serious consideration of whether it might be therapeutic for the patient. Therapists are to be pitied if they have to resort to their patients for their own sexual fulfillment, not to mention that the patients in this kind of a situation are being badly taken advantage of and may even suffer severe psychological trauma as a result. If and when an analyst proposes to sleep with his patient, the patient only has one alternative—"Get out for your own sake."

The families of analysts are bound to suffer since the analyst is tied to a rather rigid schedule. Many analysts have to work during the evenings, as most patients are not always able to come to daytime sessions. So analysts must have patient and understanding wives, not to mention children, who often feel neglected, as perhaps the wives do also.

Planning is an important part of the life of an analyst. He cannot spontaneously decide to take off on the spur of the moment, but as mentioned earlier must plan vacations and even long weekends far in advance since any slight change in schedule might upset the patient.

Are analysts getting rich? There are often-told tales about rich analysts charging enormous fees and hiding their profits away in Switzerland. Amusing but rarely true. To begin with, the average analyst begins his actual career rather late in life. After getting an M.D. or Ph.D. or other graduate degree, he has to enter a psychoanalytic training institute to start his formal analytic training: in most cases this takes anywhere from three to five years. The cost of this kind of training is considerable since, having completed and paid for his own personal analysis, he now has to be supervised by training analysts, at great expense and as often as three or four times a week, especially in the first years of practice.

When an analyst finally starts out in private practice he might charge from $25 to $50 (there are, of course, analysts who charge $50 and $75, but those are rare). With a patient load of, say, thirty sessions a week, which is considered quite taxing, he might make a gross income of $1,000 a week. But after the Internal Revenue Service takes its share and he has paid his high insurance fees, he is not all that well off. Patients often forget that if an analyst should become ill he does not get paid at all (this is one of the reasons he must carry heavy insurance), nor does he get paid when he goes on vacation. His income stops whenever he takes off. While most patients are comfortably employed and enjoy the benefits of paid vacations and sick benefits, the analyst does not have that kind of security, nor does he have a pension. Consequently he must make arrangements to cover those contingencies and the cost of such arrangements figure in what he charges. It is not so strange, then, to see analysts continuing to practice until they are far into their seventies. Freud saw patients when in his eighties.

Like professionals in other fields, the analyst has to keep abreast of the times, which means that he must do a tremendous amount of reading in order to keep up with current trends. He must also attend numerous conventions and meetings where he can listen to reports of the latest developments in the field of psychoanalysis.

Some patients actually believe that their analysts will keep them in analysis forever just to make money out of them. While such instances unfortunately do occur, the great majority of analysts who keep patients in analysis for a considerable number of years have good reason to do so, and patients should realize that perhaps they need a lengthy analysis in order to maintain a satisfactory level of functioning. An analyst who must see a patient through a ten-year analysis will have a great deal of work to do in order to perform well in the analytic situation.

Taking the rather exhaustive aspects of the analytic process into consideration, it is no wonder that the analyst has to plan his life rather carefully in order to be able to take the stress involved. Comfort and relaxation are important to him, and periodically he needs to get away from the analytic situation. Freud himself traveled a great deal in the early years of his analytic practice, and insisted on long summer vacations (about three months), although, as I mentioned before, he would sometimes take along a patient or two. Little has been written on the relaxation of the analyst, but the analyst who ignores the stress and strain of his everyday practice will likely pay a high emotional and physical price in the end.

Questions have been raised about the desirability of analysts socializing with their patients. It would be a sad thing for an analyst if he were dependent on his patients for his social life. Besides all the traditional arguments against socializing with patients, one can raise the issue that it should be good for the analyst to *get away* from his patients once in a while. For that reason he will do well to avoid social contacts with them, at least for the duration of their analyses.

There is probably a great deal of socializing by analysts among themselves; this might be unavoidable at times but it is not to be recommended. Analysts more than anyone else should try to get out of their work situation in their free hours and relax with people other than their colleagues. Again it is interesting to note here that Freud socialized on Sundays with good friends who did not belong to his inner psychoanalytic circle. Analysts who talk "shop" *ad infinitum* with their colleagues risk diluting their own strength and stamina for coping with the many facets of the analytic situation.

It is sometimes said that analysts never leave their own analysis as a result of working with patients on a continuous basis. That puts an additional burden on the analyst which most patients are unaware of. Because of the very nature of his work the analyst is in close touch with his own psyche. He cannot escape it and so, more than just about any other professional, must live with his work and cope with it. Part of this process is, of course, his countertransference with his patients, but it seems to be that a larger process takes place *within* the analyst. In an interview with Adelaide Bry, Dr. Erwin Singer, a Frommian therapist, remarks that "it has often been said that the most depressed group of people are psychiatrists and psychoanalysts. I think this is a correct observation and stems from a good reason."[3] After being asked what the reason is he continues, "Because if one daily deals with the discrepancies and hypocrisies in the lives

---

[3] Adelaide Bry (ed.), *Inside Psychotherapy* (New York: Basic Books, 1972), pp. 55–56.

of others, and if you have some shred of integrity left, the discrepancies in your own life will strike you, and so I tend to be depressed about myself." Thus the analytic situation becomes a *testing ground* for the analyst himself. He is acutely aware of his own fragility. His patients tune him in on the often awesome forces of their unconsciousness and in turn of his own.

Knowing all of this about your analyst, should you still ask him questions about himself and his personal life? If your analyst has been trained in the conventional school of analysis he certainly will not involve himself in a discussion of his life but will examine your questions in terms of yours. If he is a more involved (*engagé*) analyst, more existentially oriented, he will certainly deal with your questions in terms of himself; but he, too, will relate them to you, though with less reluctance on his part to discuss matters of a personal nature.

An analyst who has been trained in the orthodox fashion will usually be (and most of the time is) able to hide his own feelings from his patients. Any crisis in his life will pass you by and he will never reveal his own anxieties. Patients in the analytic situation are apt to pick up a disturbance in their analyst, however, and most of them tend to confront the analyst with it. He might look sick or tired, he might be yawning behind his hand or somewhat restless.

Of course if your analyst is faced with a severe crisis in his life such as a death in his family, for example, there is no way for him to hide this. And most, if not all, analysts will reveal to you the cause of the interruption in therapy. It is interesting that most patients will associate to events in the life of their analysts. A skillful analyst will then use this information to continue with your associations rather than stay with his own problem.

But not only crises in the analyst's life figure in your analysis; there are also crises in the world, and any major world crisis will bring a reaction from you and in turn from your analyst. I remember vividly the day President Kennedy was shot, and the reactions of many patients to that event. Although I did not initiate any discussion of the event, most of my patients did. Some would say, "How can I talk about my silly problems, when this has just happened." Others expressed their genuine grief and asked how I felt about it. Since I am an existentially oriented analyst, I shared my feelings with those patients and indicated that I, too, was upset by this terrible happening and that in such instances *grief* is very important as a therapeutic tool. Those who did not react and who went on talking about themselves as if nothing happened were in my opinion the most alienated and disturbed of my patients. They were so involved and caught up in their own little worlds that they had lost the ability to relate meaningfully to what happened in the larger world outside.

Often the question is raised, "Can I talk with my analyst about things other than my problems?" Orthodox analysts will state that you can talk about anything that comes to your mind but that such material has to be related to your being in analysis, and that all of the material you produce has to be analyzed.

However, some analysts in the modern progressive schools feel that they can and should discuss subjects with patients that are not necessarily related to the patient's analysis. They might discuss a play, a movie, politics, literature, and other subjects of mutual interest. The orthodox school of analysis probably will view bringing up such material as resistance on the part of the patient and an avoidance of talking about his real problems. Most present-day analysts, however, feel that the world is so much with us and around us that discussion of it is important in making the patient feel that he is in touch with the world.

In selecting your analyst you might give serious attention to the personality of your analyst. You might even want to know what his position is *vis-à-vis* major problems in today's society. Some patients feel very strongly about this, especially young patients who do not want a replica of their parents' views. They may carefully question the analyst on his position, for example, on race, poverty, war, drugs, and sexuality. I think those questions are valid since you are going to travel a long way with him, and you are entitled to know with whom you are traveling.

Above all you should understand that analysts on the whole are complicated persons themselves. They are not mad as many critics would have you believe, but they have their fair share of problems. Moreover, the nature of their work has made them more complex. Regardless of the benefits of their own personal analysis, they are subjected more than most people to the moods and tempers of others. They live a life of divided loyalties, again more than any other professionals, since they are committed to their patients, but also have their own personal lives and commitments. Finding a balance between you, the patient, and their own life commitment is an arduous task for an analyst, but most are fortunately able to do so.

Appendix I

THE MAIN PSYCHOANALYTIC SCHOOLS

THE FREUDIAN SCHOOL

Freudian therapy remains one of the most valid tools for the analysis of reasonably intact individuals. Admittedly, many persons today are not good candidates for Freudian analysis, since it requires not only hard work, dedication and persistence on the part of the patient, intelligence and the ability to articulate one's feelings, but also a substantial financial sacrifice.

The process is long, but for many it is well worth it. It is painful, but in the end it is often productive and rewarding.

Freudian analysis holds that the origin of neurosis is to be found in infantile sexual conflicts, and that the influence of the parents on the early development of the child is critical and must be thoroughly explored in the analysis of the patient.

Consequently, the Freudian analyst stresses the past, since he believes that the basis of the patient's present emotional difficulties lies in childhood experiences which have been repressed and relegated to the unconscious. The experiences can be made conscious again through dreams and fantasies. Freudians consider dream interpretation to be the "royal road to the unconscious."

The process takes a long time because of the intricate interplay between patient and analyst in terms of transference and countertransference. Transference is not established overnight, but grows slowly. Once it has been established it is an invaluable tool for the analyst to interpret the patient's reactions *vis-à-vis* early parent figures. The analyst will take the full load of the patient's hostility in the process, during which the patient will view the analyst as either father or mother or any other significant authority figure from his childhood. By making the patient conscious of the fact that he has irrationally transferred to the analyst attributes of and emotions felt toward these all-important parental or authority figures, the patient learns to evaluate and reinterpret objectively distorted infantile experiences which are the cause of his neurosis.

THE EXISTENTIAL-INTERPERSONAL SCHOOL

After reading the works of such existential analysts as Ludwig Binswanger and Medard Boss, many analysts will declare, "Well, I think I was an existential analyst all along!" The existential school stems from a great tradition in philosophy starting with the Danish philospher Sören Kierkegaard, whose books even today read like psychoanalytic treatises on alienation and loneliness.

Both the existential school and the interpersonal schools of analysis, as represented by Erich Fromm, Karen Horney, and Harry Stack Sullivan, are rooted in a European tradition. It is significant that personal links exist between Sándor Ferenczi, that innovative pupil of Freud; Clara Thompson, an analysand of Sándor Ferenczi and a distinguished neo-Freudian; and Erich Fromm; and that Ludwig Binswanger, the father of the existential school of psychoanalysis, cherished a lifelong friendship with Freud.

The existential and interpersonal schools of analysis do not stress the past in the patient's analysis, and they do not necessarily emphasize the sexual origin of their patients' neuroses. They emphasize the patient's present situation, his being-in-the-world. They see that the life situation (the world) of their patients is often neurotically restricted. The objective in the existential and interpersonal analysis is to free the patient from these restraints by showing him the ever-unfolding possibilities of his own being. They stress his freedom, and at the same time they point out to him that he alone is responsible for the exercise of that freedom.

In such an analysis the analyst is not a screen against which the patient projects a parental image, as in Freudian therapy, but the analyst assumes another role. He is more of a participant in the analytic process, and shares with his patient the grief and joy of the existential journey into the patient's unconscious.

It should be noted here that the techniques of the existential and interpersonal schools do not differ drastically from those of the Freudian school. They both acknowledge the existence of transference, countertransference, and resistance, although they place different emphases on them.

The interpersonal schools stress the role and influence of society on the patient's development. Adherents of this school do not see the patient as a entity separate from the society in which he lives and functions. Any dysfunction on the part of the patient is linked to his overall relationship to society. Here is the link with the existential school of thought as it has been expressed by R.D. Laing and David Cooper, who maintain that the families of their patients mirror an inadequate and impoverished society. Thus, such analysts feel that in order to treat their patients they must also somehow treat the society in which their patients live. Existential analysis does not necessarily mean a shortening of the analysis. Often an existential analysis requires as many years as an orthodox analyst.

GESTALT THERAPY

The emergence of Gestalt therapy has had tremendous impact and influence on contemporary psychoanalysis. The originator of Gestalt therapy, Fritz Perls, revolutionized many of the techniques of psychoanalysis. Gestaltists maintain that their object in treating is to "fill up the holes," as Perls once remarked. The patient is under considerable pressure in both his individual and his group therapy to *confront* the holes in his existence. Many of the traditional techniques that Freudian, existential, and interpersonal therapists still hold to have been discarded by the

Gestaltists. They stress the *immediate* need of the patient to confront his distortions and self-deceptions in the treatment situation. The Gestalt therapist, and one should read Perls' works to see illustrations of this, is by and large an aggressive therapist who will not take no for answer. Such therapists are especially strong in the interpretation (a term they would not like to use) of dreams and fantasies, and they have done some of the most important work on dream material during the last decade.

THE BIO-ENERGETIC SCHOOL

The bio-energetic approach to psychoanalysis stems from a proud tradition initiated by Wilhelm Reich. It holds, and justifiably so, that the body has been ignored in traditional analysis. Thus bio-energetic analysts stress the body in the analytic process. They view body posture, body expressions, and body movements as illustrations of the patient's emotional state of health. Consequently, in their treatment they stress the importance and meaning of the patient's bodily gestures. They emphasize massage and relaxation, as well as physical aggression by the patient in the therapist's office—the beating of pillows with tennis rackets, for example. This approach, combined with some of the traditional tools of psychoanalysis, has proved to be quite successful and productive for many contemporary patients who are ill at ease in their own bodies. By helping the patient to relax and be at ease with his body, the patient is free to examine his emotional problems more closely.

Appendix II

WHERE TO GO FOR
HELP IN FINDING AN ANALYST

It is not enough to know what kind of therapist or analyst you should see; you should also know *where to go* to find one. Quite a few people go to their family physician and ask him for advice. If you ask your family doctor for assistance, most of the time you will end up with a psychiatrist, since most medical doctors refer patients only to other M.D.'s. If you are interested in a psychoanalyst rather than a psychiatrist, you will do best to contact any of the training institutes that might exist in your city or the city nearest your home. In New York, for example, there is the New York Psychoanalytic Society (highly orthodox and limited to medical psychoanalysts) the William Alanson White Institute (neo-Freudian; lay and medical analysts); the National Psychological Association for Psychoanalysis (NPAP; primarily lay analysts, somewhat orthodox in orientation); the Post-Graduate Center for Psychotherapy (lay and medical analysts, eclectic in orientation); and the American Institute for Psychotherapy and Psychoanalysis (AIPP; primarily lay analysts, eclectic in orientation). All of these institutes will be able to refer you to any of their affiliated analysts. They can also often refer you to their students-in-training, who will treat you at a reduced fee. Since these trainees have supervision you do not run any risk in selecting one of them as an analyst. Moreover, sometimes young analysts work harder at their job and are more enthusiastic about it than some of the older, established analysts.

In larger cities such as New York there are other facilities available, such as some of the family-counseling centers. In New York the Jewish Board of Guardians will refer you to a properly qualified therapist. One of the largest and most well-known of the referral clinics in New York is the Community Guidance Service, which offers low-cost therapy with any of their 300 staff therapists. They are quite eclectic in their orientation, and offer a wide choice of therapeutic approaches.

Of course, New York and other large cities have the advantage of having training institutes. If you live in a smaller city you might have to depend on friends who have been or are in therapy themselves for referrals. This type of referral is also quite common in larger cities where analysands or former analysands refer their friends to their analysts.

Most universities have counseling programs (often called departments of counseling, and sometimes housed in the dean of students office), and they usually have a list of psychotherapists available. Students who want psychotherapy often use that route for securing therapy. In small communities you may have to depend on the general practitioner, who might be able to refer you to a nearby psychologist, psychoanalyst, or psychiatrist. If nothing works out you can write directly to the American Psychological Association, 1200 Seventeenth Street, N.W., Washington, D.C. 20036, and ask them to provide you with a list of clinical psychologists in or near your community.

In large cities the underprivileged have greater access to psychotherapy than anywhere else. Most hospitals maintain outpatient clinics and will refer those who are in need of psychotherapy to an appropriate psychotherapist. In most cities in the United States there are various social work agencies that often can provide you with a list of psychotherapists, as can some of the religiously affiliated agencies, and sometimes even the churches themselves.

If you can afford a reasonable fee, your best bet is a private referral, because most of the time the friend who is referring the therapist to you will recommend that therapist because he knows about his work—and results!

Bibliography

SELECTED READINGS

ANDREAS-SALOME, LOU. *The Freud Journal of Lou Andreas-Salome.* New York: Basic Books, 1964.

BOSS, MEDARD. *Psychoanalysis and Daseinsanalysis.* New York: Basic Books, 1963.

BRY, ADELAIDE, ed. *Inside Psychotherapy.* New York: Basic Books, 1972

COOPER, DAVID. *The Death of the Family.* New York: Pantheon, 1970.

————. *The Grammar of Living.* New York: Pantheon, 1974.

FERENCZI, SÁNDOR. *Further Contributions to the Theory and Technique of Psychoanalysis.* New York: Basic Books, 1960.

FOUCAULT, MICHEL. *The Birth of the Clinic.* New York: Vintage, 1975.

Bibliography

FREUD, SIGMUND, *The Interpretation of Dreams*, Vols. IV & V., The Complete Psychological Works of Sigmund Freud. London: Hogarth Press, The Standard Edition, 1953

————. *Papers on Technique*. Collected Papers, Vol II, New York: Basic Books, 1959

————. *The Question of Lay Analysis*. Vol. XX, The Standard Edition, London: Hogarth Press, 1959.

————. "Analysis Terminable and Interminable," Vol. XXIII. The Standard Edition, London: Hogarth Press, 1959.

————. *The Origins of Psychoanalysis*. Letters to Wilhelm Fliess. New York: Doubleday Anchor, 1957.

GUNTRIP, HARRY. *Schizoid Phenomena, Object-Relations and the Self*. London: The Hogarth Press, 1968

HORNEY, KAREN. *Self-Analysis*. New York; Norton, 1942.

JAFFE, DENNIS T., ed. *In Search of a Therapy*. New York: Harper, 1975.

KHAN, M. MASUD R. *The Privacy of the Self*. New York: International Universities Press, 1974.

LOWEN, ALEXANDER. *The Betrayal of the Body*. New York: Macmillan, 1967.

MACNAB, FRANCIS A. *Estrangement and Relationship.* London: Tavistock Publications, 1965.

MALAN, D.H. *A Study of Brief Psychotherapy.* London: Tavistock Publications, 1963.

MAY, ROLLO, ed. *Existence.* New York: Basic Books, 1958.

MENNINGER, KARL. *Theory of Psychoanalytic Technique.* New York: Basic Books, 1958.

MITCHELL, JULIET. *Psychoanalysis and Feminism.* New York: Pantheon, 1974.

MULLAHY, PATRICK. *The Contributions of Harry Stack Sullivan.* New York: Hermitage House, 1952.

NIN, ANAÏS. *The Diary of Anaïs Nin.* Vol. I. New York: Harcourt Brace Jovanovich, Inc. 1966.

PERLS, FREDERICK S. *Gestalt Therapy Verbatim.* Lafayette (Cal.): Real People Press, 1969.

RACKER, HEINRICH. *Transference and Counter-Transference.* New York: International Universities Press, 1968.

RANK, OTTO. *The Myth of the Birth of the Hero.* New York: Vintage, 1959.

REICH, WILHELM. *Character Analysis.* New York: Noonday Press, 1967.

RUITENBEEK, HENDRIK M. *Psychoanalysis and Existential Philosophy.* New York: Dutton, 1963.

————. *Freud and America.* New York: Macmillan, 1966.

————, ed. *Going Crazy.* New York: Bantam, 1972.

————, ed. *The Analytic Situation.* Chicago: Aldine, 1973.

————, ed. *Freud As We Knew Him.* Detroit: Wayne State University Press, 1973.

SHAPIRO, DAVID. *Neurotic Styles.* New York: Basic Books, 1965.

SIMKIN, JAMES S. *Mini-Lectures in Gestalt Therapy.* Albany, Cal:. Wordpress, 1974.

STROUSE, JEAN, ed. *Women & Analysis.* New York: Viking, 1974.

SULLIVAN, HARRY STACK. *The Psychiatric Interview.* New York: Norton, 1954

SZASZ, THOMAS S. *The Ethics of Psychoanalysis.* New York: Basic Books, 1965.

THOMPSON, CLARA M. *Interpersonal Psychoanalysis.* New York: Basic Books, 1964.

WINNICOTT, D. W. *Collected Papers.* London: Tavistock Publications, 1958.

WOLBERG, LEWIS R. *Short-Term Psychotherapy*. New
York: Grune & Stratton, 1965.

WOLSTEIN, BENJAMIN. *Counter-Transference*. New
York: Grune & Stratton, 1959.

INDEX

Abraham, Karl, 69 n, 129
Acting out, 44, 87-8, 92, 93-5, 123
Active therapy, 45, 52, 59, 106
Advice, 60
Affect, 95
Alexander, Franz, 111
Alienation, 125
American Academy of Psychotherapists, 127
American Group Psychotherapy Association, 120, 127
American Institute for Psychotherapy and Psychoanalysis, 27, 147
American Psychoanalytic Association, 27
American Psychological Association, 127, 149
Analysis Terminable and Interminable, 2, 152
Analytic group therapy, 122, 124-5
Analytic psychotherapy, 18-20
Analyst as father, 100
Analytic Situation, The, 67 n, 154
Andreas-Salome, Lou, 151
Anxiety, 28, 38, 73, 74; separation, 114-16
"The Argument Against Required Personal Analysis in Training for Psychotherapy", 129 n

Balint, Michael, 52
Betrayal of the Body, 152
Binswanger, Ludwig, 142
Bio-energetic group therapy, 126
Birth of the Clinic, 151
Body, the, 145
Boss, Medard, 54-8, 62, 71-7, 142, 151; attitude toward patient, 57-8; dreams, 71-7; on lying down, 54-6; treatment, 62
Bry, Adelaide, 90-3, 135, 151
Bulletin of the Menninger Clinic, 67 n

Castration dreams, 78
Chemotherapy, 17, 28
Clinical Papers and Essays on Psychoanalysis, 69 n
Character Analysis, 153
Character of the therapist, 35-6, 46, 129-32, 138-9. *See also* Problems of the Therapist; Countertransference
Clinics. *See* Institutes
Collected Papers (Winnicott), 154
Community Guidance Service, 148
Community oriented therapy, 17
Compulsive behavior, 71-2
Confidentiality, 125
Conflict, 90

Index

Consciousness-raising group therapy, 126
"Constructions in Analysis", 15
Contributions of Harry Stack Sullivan, 63 n, 153
Cooper, David, 144, 151
Couch. *See* Lying down
Counter-Transference, 155
Countertransference, 16, 20, 37, 88, 94, 98-9, 135, 142, 143-4; negative, 99; positive, 99. *See also* Problems of the therapist
Creativity, 125
Crisis therapy, 17
Cure, 21, 23-4, 93, 108-9. *See also* Half-cured patient
Daseinsanalysis, 55-8
Death of the Family, The, 151
Dependency, 110-1
Depth analysis, 20, 126
Depth-psychology, 29
Diagnosis, 103
Diary of Anaïs Nin, The, 46 n, 153
"Discontinuous Analyses", 106-107
Displacement, 91
Doolittle, Hilda, 37
Dreams, 68-84, 113-4, 141; actual content of, 71, 78; castration, 78; distortion of, 69; Freudian interpretation of, 71, 74; group dream seminars, 79; interpretation of, 16, 17, 18, 29, 34; latent content of, 71, 78, 79; manifest content of, 71; transference, 75
Drugs, 28

Ego, 64
Emotional immaturity, 93
Emotions, 92, 94
Encounter therapy, 17, 25
Esalen, 79
Estrangement and Relationships, 153
Ethical motives, 97
Ethics of Psychoanalysis, 154
Existence, 153

Existential analysis, 20, 24, 54-8, 60, 62, 71-5, 79-84, 92-4, 96, 122, 136, 142-4

Feces, 72
Feelings of therapist. *See* Countertransference; Problems of the therapist
Fees, 20, 32, 34, 114, 121, 131-3, 148
Female analyst, 31
Fenichel, Otto, 16
Ferenczi, Sándor, 17, 45, 57, 57 n, 106, 106 n, 109, 109 n, 111, 143, 151
First sessions(s), 38, 39-41, 51, 53-4, 64-5
Fixated libido, 62
Fixation, 82
Foucault, Michel, 151
Fragmentation, 82
Free association, 84, 122
Freud and America, 154
Freud As We Knew Him, 154
Freud Journal of Lou Andreas-Salome, 151
Freud, Sigmund, 15-6, 17, 20, 23, 24, 28-30, 33, 37, 40-1, 42-3, 44-5, 52, 53-4, 57-8, 68, 69-71, 74, 78, 87-8, 89, 90, 92-3, 94, 95, 97-9, 101, 104, 105-6, 112, 116, 129, 130, 133, 134, 135, 141-2; on dreams, 68, 69-71, 89; on psychoanalytic process, 33, 40-1 42-3, 53-4; on training, 29-30; on transference, 87-9, 95, 97, 98-9, 101; on transference resistance, 92-3, 94, 101; on transference of love, 97, 98-9, 101; on treatment (giving up), 104-5, (interruption of), 105-6 (length of) 104, 105-6, (termination of), 112. Works: "Analysis Terminable and Interminable", 15, 112; "Constructions in Analysis", 15; "The Dynamics of Transference", 52 n; "Fragment of an Analysis of a Case of Hysteria", 89 n; *A General Introduction*

to *Psychoanalysis*, 88 n; "The Handling of Dream-Interpretation", 69-71; *The Interpretation of Dreams*, 15, 23; "Observations on Transference-Love", 87 n, 97-9, 101; "On Beginning the Treatment", 40-41, 53-4, 104; *The Question of Lay Analysis*, 28 n, 152; "Remembering, Repeating and Working-Through", 92-3; *Three Contributions to the Theory of Sex*, 15

Freudian analyst, 75
Fromm, Erich, 135, 142, 143
"The Further Development of an Active Therapy in Psychoanalysis", 106 n
Further Contributions to the Theory and Technique of Psychoanalysis, 57 n, 61, 109, 151

Gestalt group therapy, 125
Gestalt therapy, 49, 79-84, 107, 125
Gestalt Therapy Verbatim, 79-84, 153
Ghetto therapy, 18
Going Crazy, 154
Grammar of Living, 151
Greenson, Ralph, 16
Group therapy, 119-27; socializing with members of, 123-4
Guilt, 44, 72-3
Guntrip, Harry, 152

Half-cured patient, 109
Hammett, Dr., 90-3
Heterosexual analysts, 32
Holt, Robert R., 129 n
Homosexual analysts, 32
Homosexual Community Counseling Center, 32
Homosexuals, 32
Horney, Karen, 142, 152

Identity, 125
In Search of a Therapy, 152
Incest, 124

In-depth therapy, 105
Infantile fixations, 94, 97, 141
Inhibitions, 93
Inside Psychotherapy, 92n, 135 n, 151
International Psychoanalytic Association, 25
Interpersonal Psychoanalysis, 154
Interpersonal relationships, 113
Intervention therapy, 17
Interruption of therapy, 103-4, 105, 107, 113
Institutes: American Institute of Psychotherapy and Psychoanalysis, 27, 147; American Psychological Association, 127, 149; Community Guidance Service, 148; National Psychological Association for Psychoanalysis, 27, 147; New York Psychoanalytic Society, 147; Post Graduate Center for Psychotherapy, 27, 147; William Alanson White Institute, 27, 147
Interpretation of Dreams, The, 15, 23, 152
Involvement of therapist. *See* Countertransference

Jaffe, Dennis T., 152
Jewish Board of Guardians, 148
Jones, Ernest, 15
Journal of the American Psychoanalytic Association, 88
Jung, Carl, 72, 73, 74

Kennedy, John F., 137
Khan, M. Masud, 67 n, 152
Kierkegaard, Sören, 142

Laing, R. D., 144
Lay analysts, 25-30. *See also* Qualifications
Leader, Arthur L., 129 n
Lesbians, 125
Love, 94, 97-9
Love object, 87-8, 94
Lowen, Alexander, 152
Lying down, 53-7

Index

MacNab, Francis A., 153
Maintenance therapy, 110
Malan, D. H., 153
Marital therapy, 30
May, Rollo, 153
Mini-Lectures in Gestalt Therapy, 154
Menninger Clinic, Bulletin of the, 67 n
Menninger, Karl, 16, 111, 153
Missed appointments, 20, 25, 104-6, 107
Mitchell, Juliet, 153
Mullahy, Patrick, 153
Myth of the Birth of the Hero, 153

National Psychological Association for Psychoanalysis, 27, 147
Negative transference, 41, 96, 99
Neo-Freudian, 20, 24, 27
Neurosis, 73, 88-9, 93
Neurotic behavior, 92-3
Neurotic Styles, 154
Neurotics, 24
New Group Therapies, The, 126 n
New Horizons for Psychotherapy, 129 n
New York Psychoanalytic Society, 147
Nin, Anaïs, 45-6, 153

Origins of Psychoanalysis, The, 152
Orr, D., 88-9

Papers on Technique, 152
Patient, the, 25, 47-52, 62-5, 71-3, 107, 115. *See also* Half-cured patient
Penis, 78
Perls, Fritz, 79-83, 144-5, 153
Permissiveness, 95
Phallic symbols, 72
Phantasies, 106, 141, 145
Post Graduate Center for Psychotherapy, 27, 147
Privacy of the Self, The, 152

Problems of the therapist, 130-2, 135-7. *See also* Countertransference
Problem-solving, 25
Problem-solving group therapy, 125-6
Process of psychoanalysis, 18
Projection, 82-3, 124, 131
Psychiatric Interview, The, 154
Psychiatry, 18
Psychoanalysis, 15-7, 19-20, 23-4; in America, 17; as distinct from Psychotherapy, 23-4
Psychoanalysis and Daseinsanalysis, 55 n, 56 n, 58 n, 62 n, 151
Psychoanalysis and Existential Philosophy, 154
Psychoanalysis and Feminism, 153
Psychoanalytic establishment, the, 28
Psychoanalytic Schools: Bioenergetic, 145; Existential-Interpersonal, 142-4; Freudian, 141-2; Gestalt, 144-5
Psychology, 18, 26
Psychoses, 24
Psychotherapy, 20, 23-6
Psychotic episode, 72

Qualifications of the therapist, 18-9, 26-8, 39-42, 49, 120, 127, 132
Question of Lay Analysis, The, 28 n, 152

Racker, Heinrich, 153
Rank, Otto, 17, 45-6, 78-9, 116, 129, 153
Regression, 88
Reich, Wilhelm, 145, 153
Reik, Theodore, 27
Religious symbols, 72
Repression, 20, 67-8
Repressed feeling (repressed emotions), 52-3, 87, 94
Resistance, 20, 52, 57, 69, 73, 94, 101, 104, 105, 109, 122, 138, 144

Responsibility, 77-8
"The Role of Personal Psycho-
therapy in the Training of
Psychotherapists", 129 n
Rubinfine, David L., 129 n
Ruitenbeek, Hendrik, 21, 67 n,
154

*Schizoid Phenomena, Object-Re-
lations and the Self*, 152
Selecting an analyst/therapist,
20, 25, 27-38, 46, 138. *See also*
Institutes of Psychiatry; Quali-
fications
Self-Analysis, 152
Sensitivity group therapy, 126
Sex: and money, 45; with mem-
bers of group, 123-4; with the
therapist, 36, 98-9, 131
Sexual dysfunctioning, 123; per-
formance, 113; symbolism, 78
Shame, 73
Shapiro, David, 154
Short-term therapy, 106, 107,
126
Short-Term Psychotherapy, 155
"Should Patients Write Down
Their Dreams", 69 n
"Silence As Communication",
67 n
Simkin, James S., 154
Singer, Erwin, 135
Socializing with patients, 134-5
Sociology, 18, 27
Stopping therapy, 105-6
Strachey, James, 15
Strouse, Jean, 154
Study of Brief Psychotherapy, A,
153
Subjects for discussion, 137-8
Sublimation, 95

Suitable candidate for therapy,
24-5
Suitable treatment for patient, 64
Sullivan, Harry Stack, 46-8, 59-
60, 63, 142
Sullivan and Treatment, 47 n,
59 n
Supportive therapy, 107
Symptom solving, 25
Szasz, Thomas S., 154

Talkativeness, 57, 59
Termination of therapy, 110-7
Theme-oriented group therapy,
125
*Theory of Psychoanalytic Tech-
nique*, 153
Thompson, Clara M., 143, 154
Training. *See* Qualifications
Transference, 20, 30, 31, 33,
36-7, 52, 54, 65, 75, 78, 85,
87-90, 91-103, 109, 122, 142,
143; dependency, 115; negative, 96-7, 99-101; positive,
96-7, 99-101
*Transference and Countertrans-
ference*, 153
Tribute to Freud (Hilda Doolittle), 37 n

White, Mary Julian, 47 n, 48 n,
59 n, 60 n
William Alanson White Insti-
tute, 27, 147
Winnicott, D. W., 154
Wolberg, Lewis R., 155
Wolf Man, 106, 116
Wolstein, Benjamin, 155
Women & Analysis, 154
Women's Liberation, 31
Working through, 95